Drawing for Illustration

Martin Salisbury

Drawing for
Illustration

Introduction

'One of the difficulties inherent in
using words to write or speak about
drawing is the fact that, ultimately,
drawing is itself a language'

Drawing remains the fundamental language of the illustrator, and an equally fundamental aspect of illustration's research and preparation. In its many guises and meanings, 'drawing' continues to feed and underpin the output of the successful illustrative artist, even if it is not the actual method used to create the work. It is drawing, and the understanding or 'knowing' that it nurtures, which informs convincing illustrative image-making in all its forms.

In 1962 the illustrator and painter Lynton Lamb published *Drawing for Illustration* with Oxford University Press. It was an important contribution to the understanding of the illustrator's art and craft at the time. Analysis of the various print processes through which illustrators' original artworks found their way to the printed page inevitably formed a significant proportion of Lamb's text, as did the need to be able to work to a particular scale. From the invention of printing until around the time when Lamb wrote his text, it had been paramount for illustrators to have a full understanding of these processes. In shamelessly stealing the title of Lamb's excellent book, I hope to further illuminate the subject in the context of today's publishing industries, in a world much changed.

This is not strictly speaking an instructional book, and it is certainly not one that reveals miraculous tricks or short-cuts, but the aim is nevertheless that it may help students and others to develop their drawing specifically in relation to the art of illustration, while also gaining some broader insights into historical context. It is important to stress at the outset that I do not believe there is a particular 'way' of drawing for illustration, certainly not in the stylistic sense. But there are certain differences in approach to drawing between, on the one hand, the narrative or interpretative artist and on the other, the formal analytical draughtsman.

One of the difficulties inherent in using words to write or speak about drawing is the fact that, ultimately, drawing is itself a language. As the illustrator and painter John Minton pointed out in his lecture 'Speculations on the Contemporary Painter'(City of Birmingham Scool of Painting, 1952), 'a Cézanne cannot be *described*, if it could there would have been no need for it to have been painted'. The language of drawing goes beyond description. In *The Use of Poetry and the Use of Criticism* (Faber, 1937), T. S. Eliot, writing about poetry rather than drawing, speculated that the

---

P. 2: Yann Kebbi, *Mouvement*.
P. 4: A sheet of developmental studies for narrative book illustrations by Charles Edmund Brock.

OPPOSITE: A preparatory sketch and final printed illustration by H. M. Brock from Oliver Wendell Holmes's *Breakfast Table* series, books of essays published in the early 1900s.

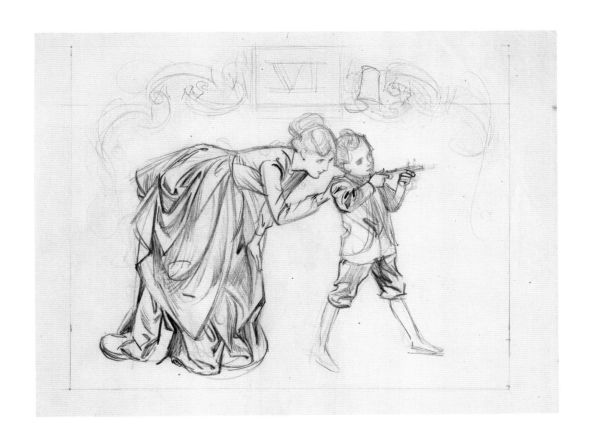

chief use of 'meaning' in this context is often '*to satisfy one habit of the reader, to keep his mind diverted and quiet, while the poem does its work upon him: much as the imaginary burglar is always provided with a nice piece of meat for the house-dog.*' It was an idea that the philosopher Marshall McLuhan famously developed: '*For the "content" of a medium is like the juicy piece of meat carried by the burglar to distract the watchdog of the mind*', which he condensed into the phrase '*the medium is the message*'. There are clear parallels between the languages of poetry and drawing, each being formally subject to certain underlying mechanics or 'grammar', but (with the exception of purely technical or informational drawing) with 'meaning' being readable in a variety of ways.

When Lamb wrote *Drawing for Illustration*, the relationship between drawing and illustration was perhaps more straightforward than it is now. In many ways, illustration *was* drawing. Certainly, most published illustration was originally executed in ink on paper. Drawing formed the basis of teaching in the art schools of the day, in all fields of the 'fine' and applied arts. For the illustrator, these acquired skills were largely employed in making visual the writer's text, at a time when illustration was generally seen as entirely subordinate to the written word.

In the twenty-first century, illustration's connection to both formal drawing and the written word have changed considerably. Illustrators are increasingly creating their own content as graphic novelists, picturebook-makers, documentary artists: 'picture-writers', if you will. The teaching of drawing in the most formal, academic sense is, however, increasingly rare. Until relatively recently it had been seen as the foundation stone of learning across all of the visual arts. Now, in the absence of such formal training, the relationship between drawing and the activity of illustration varies greatly from one illustrator to another.

The relationship between fine art and illustration has itself long been a prickly one. In his book, Lamb quoted John Berger's famous observation that 'drawing without searching equals illustration'. Berger was referring to the most literal definition of the word, but illustration has always been easy game for such put-downs, possibly more so in recent times as fine art has moved away from any direct relationship with formal drawing skills and has therefore perhaps needed to find other ways to identify itself as of a higher purpose.

The vacuum in drawing-based expressive art is being filled by the growth in authorial visual narrative texts, as practised by a generation of expressive artist–authors such as Isabelle Arsenault, Jillian Tamaki, Shaun Tan, Isabel Greenberg, John Broadley, Jon McNaught and Brian Selznick. And, of course, the great works by children's picturebook-makers are becoming increasingly recognized within literature and the arts.

Examining the various ways in which the process and activity of drawing underpins, directs and supports the work of such artists as these, as well as their historical predecessors, is the key theme of this book.

OPPOSITE: Lynton Lamb's 1962 book *Drawing for Illustration* examined the practical and conceptual skills of the illustrator at a time when they needed to work much more closely with the craftsmen responsible for reproducing their work. FOLLOWING SPREAD: Stanley Badmin was a prolific and influential illustrator and tutor throughout much of the twentieth century. Badmin was known for the intensity of detail in his work, much of which focused on the English landscape. For this 1959 Christmas card design, *Christmas Week, Trafalgar Square*, his pencil rough appears to include preliminary colour tests for the dark night sky.

Introduction

CHAPTER 1

Drawing and Illustration

Drawing:
What is it?

'Learning to think visually is
the key to learning to draw'

As with so many areas of the creative arts, arriving at a precise definition of 'drawing' is challenging and, perhaps, ultimately not entirely meaningful. Definitions usually include get-out clauses or qualifications, because the boundaries between drawing and painting, for example, are inevitably porous. Attempts to tie down the word can easily become either too inclusive or too exclusive. And, after all, artists are not known primarily for their interest in following rules or being bound by conventions or definitions. Nevertheless, if we take the Tate's simple, pragmatic definition, we can build outwards from it:

> Drawing is essentially a technique in which images are depicted on a surface by making lines, though drawings can also contain tonal areas, washes and other non-linear marks.

Purposely avoiding straying into debate about at what point (if at all) random or accidental mark-making becomes 'drawing', my own best efforts at defining drawing for illustration quickly become cumbersome:

> Making intentional marks on a surface or through digital media to represent and communicate a physical entity or an idea (or both).

The etymology of the word itself is rooted in the physical act of *drawing* (dragging or pulling) an implement through or across the sand or soil, thereby leaving a trace or trail. The word for drawing in other languages often has completely different origins. In French and Italian, *to draw* and *drawing* are expressed through the equivalent of the English word 'design' – *dessiner* and *dessin* in French, *disegnare* and *disegno* in Italian – seemingly evolved through focus on the planning and compositional aspects of drawing.

Coming to terms with the idea of drawing as a form of language is important. Indeed, when learning to draw (which first of all necessitates learning to see), one of the most powerful impediments to progress is the brain's insistent habit of trying to change *seeing* into words. Learning to think visually is the key to learning to draw. This is one of the reasons why we sometimes hear teachers of drawing suggest that drawing from observation is less about learning and more about *unlearning*.

It may be worthwhile at this point to remind ourselves of how casually we take for granted our ability to make the connection between a simple line drawing of a thing, and the three-dimensional thing itself. After all, we don't all walk around with outlines around us. How did we learn to make the huge and complex leap of the imagination that requires us to perceive a representation of reality in the artifice of a linear contour that describes where one thing ends and another begins? Some have argued that this must be an inherent ability in humans. However, as the painter and art educationalist Richard Carline noted in his 1968 book *Draw They Must* (Edward Arnold Ltd), not all human beings have an innate ability to 'read' a representational drawing. It has been suggested

Какво правиш? – Рисувам! – Ама не мога, че ме иструвай от Интернол!
От 20 години се познаваме.
Шишката как си го нобрала...
Изваме тука всеки ден. – Всеки ден? – Всеки ден.

that the idea of representation through outline may have its origins in the particular ancient cave drawings of early man that were executed by placing one hand flat against the cave wall and using the other to trace a line around the fingers.

Wherever the origins of the human impulse to draw lie, it seems clear that it is powerful from a very early age. Very young children will 'draw' long before they have command of the spoken word.

They will continue to do so naturally and without inhibition until they reach an age when they first become conscious of notions of 'good' and 'bad' drawing, or the sense of being judged on levels of representational realism. It is sadly at this point that many children, unless they are fortunate enough to receive continued encouragement, stop drawing. Pablo Picasso's oft-quoted observation that 'It took me four years to paint like Raphael, but

---

ABOVE: This sketchbook drawing of card players in Sofia, Bulgaria, by Vyara Boyadjieva is executed almost entirely in outline, yet we are able to read it clearly in terms of space and 'who is in front of whom'.
FOLLOWING PAGE: Paintings by early humans in caves such as those at Lascaux in France or Cueva de las Manos

(Cave of the Hands) in Patagonia, Santa Cruz, Argentina, shown here, frequently include the stencilling of hands as well as multiple representations of the wild animals on which they preyed. Although there are many theories about the 'purpose' of the drawings, humankind's longstanding impulse to graphically represent the three-dimensional world is evident.

a lifetime to paint like a child' may have contained more than a little sophistry, but it does touch on the important matter of the relationships between concepts of skill or craft and pure unbridled expression in drawing.

Establishing a clear distinction between drawing and painting is not as simple as it might at first seem. Such a distinction cannot realistically be based on whether or not colour is used, or on particular media or materials. It is possible to draw with colour and it is possible to paint in a linear manner. Exploring this conundrum in *A Short Book About Drawing* (Quadrille, 2013), Andrew Marr quotes the German sculptor and symbolist Max Klinger, who proposed that, compared to painting, drawing has a 'freer relationship to the representable world'. Drawing is further away from the illusion of real three-dimensional space and forces us to unconsciously make connections, translate or 'fill in the gaps'. Meanwhile, Jean-Auguste-Dominique Ingres is said to have opined, 'Drawing includes three and a half quarters of the content of painting...drawing contains everything, except the hue'.

Each and every person will draw in their own unique way, whether trained or untrained. Every mark made speaks differently – from nervous, tentative, searching strokes to bold, gestural and direct mark-making, sometimes all in the same image. Every little change in pressure or direction will have a bearing on the character of each mark, in the same way that variation in emphasis from *pianissimo* to *fortissimo* will convey different meanings and experiences in orchestral music. Even where an artist has been taught to draw in a rigorously academic manner, aspects of their own personality, temperament and particular visual interests will force their way through and be made manifest in the nature of the marks made. This process of examining, exploring and questioning the visual world requires intense concentration.

OPPOSITE: This sketchbook sheet of observational studies of a clothed male figure was produced by an unknown art student in the 1950s. The hesitancy and constant reassessment evident in the student's line speaks of the sense of inquiry that is so important when learning to draw.

FOLLOWING SPREAD: Observational drawing has not only been the skill underpinning many painters' processes, but the technical means by which an original design was scaled up onto canvas for painting, as seen here in Walter Sickert's drawing and final painting, *Ennui* (1914). The pencil underdrawing can be clearly seen in the sketch.

Drawing and Illustration

Illustration: What is it?

'The general standing of illustration as
an art form has fluctuated over the years,
drifting repeatedly in and out of fashion'

Given the changing role and status of illustration in recent years, the question 'what is illustration?' may be as difficult to pin down as 'what is drawing?' Traditionally, dictionary definitions have focused on the role of illustration in explaining or elucidating, augmenting information that is primarily conveyed by the written word. This aspect of illustration's role remains an important one, especially in fields such as technical and informational illustration. But as illustration and fine or 'high' art grew further and further apart through the second half of the twentieth century (with certain notable exceptions), many artists, whose work was rooted in drawing and narrative and who wished to express their own concepts and ideas in primarily visual form, found a home in authorial, sequential visual work for reproduction. It is perhaps this latter aspect that is the key to defining the word 'illustration'.

Prior to the invention of printing, artists created illuminated manuscripts by hand, delicately rendering word and image as a unified whole. They saw their activity in holistic terms, as one of creating a book, rather than assigning distinct roles of 'writer' and 'illustrator' or 'artist'. But in the age of print, it became accepted practice to label a book as 'by' the writer and to use the term 'illustrated by' in relation to the creator of the book's pictorial content. With the growing incidence of what some term 'visual text', particularly in the fast-evolving field of picture-book-making, such terminology is rapidly becoming obsolete. In the instances where the word-maker and image-maker of a picturebook are separate, they are essentially co-authors. Sometimes in these situations, a book is the original concept of the artist and a writer is commissioned to put the words together, thereby overturning the notion of image as subordinate to the written word. Increasingly, we see picturebooks that are credited as 'by' the artist alongside 'words by' the writer – a reversal of traditional accreditation. Available terminology still, however, often falls short in relation to areas of authorial visual communication such as visual journalism, political satire and editorial comment. In 1976, The World Illustration Awards began, demonstrating the increasing global reach of this art form and recognizing work in fields from advertising to children's books. Other awards have followed, notably in the field of picturebook-making – for example, the Golden Pinwheel Young Illustrators Competition, run by the China Shanghai Children's Book Fair since 2015.

OPPOSITE: Original artwork for *Washington Square* (1913) by William Glackens, showing the use of white gouache or 'body colour' to add highlights and clean away unwanted detail in preparation for photography for print.

Lynton Lamb's 1962 attempt at defining illustration, 'small drawings designed to be printed in books as a comment on the author's story', reminds us how much things have moved on (pp. 7–9). My own attempt may well become similarly dated, perhaps even more quickly: 'Imagery created, singly or in sequence, to be reproduced for mass visual communication via print or screen, with or without verbal text'. As Michael Lobel points out in his book John Sloan: Drawing on Illustration (Yale University Press, 2014), it may be more useful to think of the word as an activity, rather than a thing. Identifying the purpose behind the making of the image and examining illustration as a profession may be more meaningful than trying to locate any particular identifying visual characteristics. Lobel also notes that 'illustrators recognize that the images they create are meant to be viewed not in the original but as reproductions'.

The general standing of illustration as an art form has fluctuated over the years, drifting repeatedly in and out of fashion. Throughout the late nineteenth and twentieth centuries and into the twenty-first, editorials have presented variations on a theme, lurching from 'The End of Illustration' to, within a few years, 'The Return of Illustration', only to be followed shortly after by, for example, 'Illustration: Do we need it?' The lowest point was possibly the period around the late twentieth and early twenty-first centuries, when infatuation with the emerging technologies of Adobe Photoshop, Illustrator and the like brought into question the need for, or role of, drawing in relation to illustration. Initially, many graphic designers felt that they could take on the role of illustrator by digitally importing, altering and collaging photographic imagery. Newspapers and magazines were quickly awash with this kind of work. Attitudes to illustration, especially in traditional media, became negative and condescending. At least one leading visual communication journal at the time openly declared that it would no longer feature illustration within its pages.

In July 1996, the influential American illustrator Brad Holland proffered his own somewhat sardonic definition of the distinction between illustration and fine art in The Atlantic: 'In Commercial Art, you find out how much they're going to pay you, and then you do the work. In Fine Art, it's the other way around'. He subsequently delivered a despairing if ironic rant on the perceived status of the illustrator as 'artist' in his glossary of 'key terms' for illustrators:

'That's Not Art, That's Illustration': Almost Everybody is an artist these days. Rock and Roll singers are artists. So are movie directors, performance artists, make-up artists, tattoo artists, con artists, and rap artists. Movie stars are artists. Madonna is an artist, because she explores her own sexuality. Snoop Doggy Dogg is an artist because he explores other people's sexuality. Victims who express their pain are artists. So are guys in prison who express themselves on shirt cardboard. Even consumers are artists when they express themselves in their selection of commodities. The only people left in America who seem not to be artists are illustrators.

Holland's words must have rung true for many an illustrator in 2000. In his eyes, the illustrator was being punished for being a collaborative rather than an individualistic or self-indulgent artist. Some would call this an excessive inferiority complex. But illustration and fine art have a past.

For much of its history, illustration shared with fine art a foundation in academic drawing. But even before the two parted ways it was rarely possible for those whose primary aspirations were aimed towards the gallery wall to maintain a practice as an illustrator without undermining their credibility. Notwithstanding the mobility of mid-century British artist–illustrator–designers such as Edward Bawden, Paul Nash and John Piper, the stereotype of the illustrator as frustrated painter or fine artist clung rather tenaciously, perhaps helped by the regret expressed by artists such as Edward Hopper and N. C. Wyeth, who retrospectively played down the importance of their illustration work. Yet as Richard McLanathan observes in his introduction to The Brandywine Heritage (New York Graphic Society, 1971):

'For much of its history, illustration shared with fine art a foundation in academic drawing'

The fact of the matter is that American artists have traditionally turned their hands to a variety of tasks as practicality or fancy might dictate. The creative mind in America has never been satisfied to follow those neatly defined channels of expression which have characterized much of European art during recent centuries.

As the twenty-first century entered its second decade, it was perhaps the widening of awareness (in both public and academic arenas) of the potential for the art of children's picurebook-making and other authorial forms – ironically along with the rise of digital reading tablets – that prompted yet another switch in the fortunes of illustration. The 'Tools of Change in Publishing' conference, held on the eve of the 2011 Bologna Children's Book Fair, was notable for its dire warnings of the imminent demise of the physical children's book. Failing to heed the lessons of illustration history, speaker after speaker delivered prophesies of doom to an audience of petrified publishers, confidently asserting that unless they immediately invested in the design and production of 'picturebook apps' they would be quickly left behind. After much money was lost, that which should have been clear at the outset soon became evident: a book is a book and a game is a game. The picturebook app came and went in the same manner as the legendary CD-Rom. It was apparent that the physical book would need to 'up its game' somewhat in order to compete with digital reading, but this would primarily involve greater focus on design and production – marking out the territory of the book not just as a conveyor of information, but as a haptic, physical and all-around aesthetic experience. Thus, we find ourselves once again in something of a 'Golden Age' of book illustration and design.

ABOVE: Drawing by Michal Shalev.

'Even today, making a drawing appear on a blank
sheet of paper is a bit like magic to me'

Isabelle Arsenault
Drawing and me

Drawing has always been central to the practice of the award-winning artist Isabelle Arsenault. Here, she reflects on its place in her life and work.

Childhood
As a child, I was much impressed with my father's ability to draw. He didn't work in a very creative field but, on occasion, to entertain my brother, my sister and me, he would take out his pen from the inside pocket of his business suit and grab a piece of paper to draw on. A few lines later, a character would appear. There was something mysterious and magical about it. Like when a magician pulls a bird out of a sleeve. I believe that my interest in drawing stems from there and, through my own illustrations, I have always sought to create this kind of wonder. My father also taught me oil painting. Secretly, I always tried to impress him with my creations. It made me work hard and improve quickly. I was a fairly introverted child and I felt that drawing was

a way to show a hidden side of me, some part within that was difficult to access otherwise. Later, drawing became part of my identity. At school, I was spontaneously associated with any project that required drawing skills. This made me feel valued or special (like it was a superpower) throughout my studies and pushed me to continue on this path.

College
During my college years in fine arts, the approach was rather classical: technical drawing classes, live models, still observation and so on. It was during my university studies in Graphic Design that I had the opportunity to further explore conceptual illustration. The idea of drawing took on another meaning and found a kind of purpose. There, a drawing had to be able to communicate a message in a coherent way, to speak a clear visual language. Even today, this perspective is useful to my work, especially when it comes to visual storytelling. I also had to draw storyboards,

which taught me the use of visual sequences and how the images could work together to create a whole. We were encouraged to try different approaches and think outside the box to make our concepts unique and able to stand out.

Drawing now
Drawing is very much associated with work for me now. It's intuitive because it's something I do on a daily basis. But because every project is different, one type of drawing may come more easily to me during a certain period of time, when I am working on a project of a particular style. This is why I think it is important to maintain some form of practice outside of work, in a sketchbook for example, to exercise what I have learned and explore new avenues. It's like training between marathons. If you're not in good shape, it becomes much more difficult to perform.

_ PETIT DIMANCHE tranquille

Above and following page: Sketchbook drawings by Isabelle Arsenault.
p. 27: Developmental stages and finished page from *Collette's Lost Pet*
(Random House, 2017).

Isabelle Arsenault

Drawing and Illustration

Hé! Berthe!

Aurais-tu vu l'oiseau de Colette?
C'est une perruche. Elle est bleue
avec un peu de jaune dans le cou,
elle s'appelle Elizabeth et quand
elle chante, elle fait PRrrrrrr
Prrrr PrrrrrruiiiiiiT!

Isabelle Arsenault

Drawing and Illustration

Opposite and above: Sketchbook drawings by Isabelle Arsenault.
Following spread: Initial pencil composition (p. 30, top) and finished illustrations
from *Jane the Fox and Me* (text by Fanny Britt, Walker Books, 2014).

Isabelle Arsenault

Observation

Observational drawing is all about shapes, light and shadows and reality as we see it. Once we have mastered these concepts, it is possible to deconstruct and select what we deem relevant, adapting reality to our personal point of view. In my process, I like to pit realistically rendered elements in opposition to others that are much less so. I build up images based on knowledge and reality, then I shed the superfluous and open the door to the reader, making room for pattern. When I was young, I liked to lose myself in complex illustrations, full of details and characters. I could spend hours like that, daydreaming, looking at books or psychedelic vinyl covers. Even today, everything I see is somehow transposed into textured materials when it comes to drawing: a mass of branches on the ground becomes fine hatching, a leafy shrub turns into a series of zig-zag lines. I find this style reflects the diversity that makes our world so beautiful. But using lots of patterns can easily become overwhelming. I try to focus on what truly brings something to the image.

Planning and Execution

This is a fragile balance. At the sketch stage, I try to focus on the content and not the container. My only concern is whether the message is getting across well, if the pace is good, if the idea works. I just sketch the elements minimally in their approximate place. If I push the rendering too far, I'm afraid of setting up expectations and being stuck staying in too narrow a frame. Whereas if the sketch remains open but communicates the idea well, I can go in several different directions for the final work, and it makes me more comfortable to try different approaches, adjust things, leave room for spontaneity.

Drawing and Me

Drawing for me is still very much associated with childhood – mine, but now also that of my own children. It implies being fully in the moment. It is an act of spontaneity, a gesture of communion between the hand, the eye and the brain. When that coordination is efficient, it's exhilarating and addicting. Therefore, it is almost a meditative activity that keeps me focused on the here and now. Direct inner-observation, kind of. Drawings are often perceived as incomplete, a process step before going to a final piece. This aspect touches me. Its vulnerability makes it even more precious. Even today, making a drawing appear on a blank sheet of paper is a bit like magic to me.

ELLES SONT PARTOUT,
COMME LEURS INSULTES
GRIFFONNÉES SUR LES MURS.

Isabelle Arsenault

Drawing and
the education
of the illustrator

'Because of its perceived association with that
slippery concept, "skill" or craft, it has sometimes
struggled to find its place in academia'

Over many years of teaching drawing and illustration, I have become increasingly aware of the ways in which 'knowing' emerges over time in the process of drawing, at least initially from direct observation. Applications to art schools have traditionally involved students having to attend portfolio interviews. When asked what they felt were the relative strengths and weaknesses of their portfolio, it would often be the students whose observational drawings were the weakest who would describe drawing as an area of strength. Meanwhile, those showing greatest progress would often be the most conscious of their shortcomings. In his 1857 book *The Elements of Drawing: In Three Letters to Beginners* (Smith, Elder & Co), the Victorian artist and critic John Ruskin famously wrote:

> *I believe that (irrespective of differences in individual temper and character) the excellence of an artist, as such, depends wholly on refinement of perception, and that it is this, mainly, which a master or a school can teach…I am nearly convinced,*
> *that when once we see keenly enough, there is very little difficulty in drawing what we see; but, even supposing that this difficulty be still great, I believe that the sight is a more important thing than the drawing; and I would rather teach drawing that my pupils may learn to love Nature, than teach the looking at Nature that they may learn to draw…*

This can be seen as essentially an argument against passive drawing skills and in favour of drawings as a way of opening up visual 'knowing' and the pictorial imagination, a view also espoused by Howard Pyle, the late nineteenth-century American realist painter, illustrator, influential teacher and founder of the Howard Pyle School of Illustration Art (later termed the Brandywine School by illustrator and author Henry C. Pitz). In a stance never comfortably embraced across the various levels of educational management, Pyle further proposed that drawing and illustration stand comparison with established areas of professional education:

OPPOSITE: Traditionally, illustration was mainly taught by practising illustrators working part-time alongside their primary activities. With illustration now often taught in the environment of higher education, this vital practice has become increasingly difficult to maintain. Edward Ardizzone taught in London, at Camberwell School of Arts and Crafts and the Royal College of Art. This illustration is one of several he produced for Camberwell's jubilee publication in 1948.

Drawing and the education of the illustrator

Pictures are the creations of the imagination and not of technical facility, and that...which art students most need is the cultivation of their imagination and its direction into practical and useful channels of creation – and I hold that this is exactly in line with other kinds of professional education, whether of law, medicine, finance or physics. I would not belittle the necessity of accurate technical training. I insist upon that in my own school even more strenuously than it is insisted upon in the great art schools of the country; but I subordinate that technical training entirely to the training of the imagination.

In 1979 another influential educator, Professor Bruce Archer, who championed Design Research at the Royal College of Art in London, contributed a paper to the first volume of the journal *Design Studies* in which he argued that the well-known phrase 'The Three Rs', used in the English language to describe what are seen as the three basic skills to learn in school: reading, writing and arithmetic, was anomalous. He pointed out that reading and writing were two sides, passive and active, of the same skill – the language skill – and suggested that the third fundamental area of education should

ABOVE: Sketchbook drawings by Heera Cha, combining observation with a hint of caricature.
OPPOSITE: For much of its history, art education as a whole was built around drawing from the model in the life room. This drawing, from Cambridge School of Art archive, is by an unknown student, 1960s.

relate to the 'material culture': a level of awareness that comes from art, design, music, drama and dance. To illustrate his point, he claimed to have an elderly great-aunt who swore that the concept of the 'Three R's' should be replaced by:

Reading and writing
Reckoning and figuring
Wroughting and wrighting

He went on to explain that by 'wroughting and wrighting', his (possibly imaginary) great aunt meant 'knowing how things are brought about'. Archer speculated that 'Design' or 'Design Awareness' might best define this area of tacit knowledge, and should form the third fundamental of a rounded education.

The Royal College of Art in London, at which Archer taught, was key to the development of education in the applied arts. Indeed, the arts education system in the UK is still relatively unusual in offering Illustration as a discrete subject. The influence of the British and American art education systems is still felt in many parts of the world, but in much of Europe the specific field of Illustration as an appropriate subject for undergraduate and postgraduate-level university education has been slower to find acceptance. Similarly, in many parts of East and South-East Asia, students wishing to develop their illustration skills in a contextually informed and highly personal way will often seek to study in the UK and US.

To return to Ruskin, the ability to *see* is key to the process of drawing effectively from observation and imagination. It involves a tortuous process of learning to bypass the brain's attempts to fool us into thinking we *know* in order to listen to what the eyes are *telling* us. Richard Carline, both a senior examiner of art in schools and a painter himself, wrote in depth about this in his book *Draw They Must: A History of the Teaching and Examining of Art* (Edward Arnold, 1968). He lamented the way that art practice in schools was seen as something to be studied only by those wishing to go on to art college (this is even more the case today). He argued that it should be seen as an important element of a broad education alongside the study of English and Mathematics, echoing the philosophies of Ruskin and Pyle when writing about what drawing *is* and what it is *for*:

The main goal of art teaching is not technical proficiency or skill, as usually assumed, but the development of the visual perceptions. Perhaps the art class might gain in status by a change in name, with 'art' discarded in favour of 'vision'.

Ruskin's famous assertion that 'Fine art is that in which the hand, the head, and the heart of man go together' was referring to an art world that was much more deeply embedded in the formal skills of drawing than is the case now. With illustration being perhaps one of the last bastions of draughtsmanship as a primary tool of expression, it is more than a little at odds with the university culture it often finds itself within. Because of its perceived association with that slippery concept, 'skill' or craft, it has sometimes struggled to find its place in academia, while the appreciation and academic study of children's picturebooks has tended, perhaps perversely, to fall

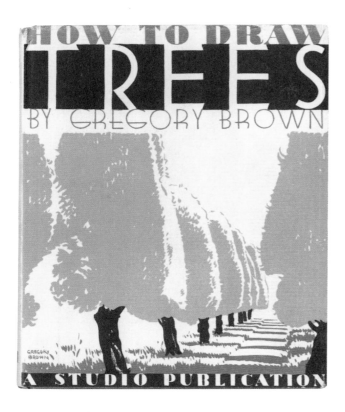

within the fields of literature and education studies. In these contexts, the motivations, intentions and 'meanings' of artists' works can be easily misunderstood or replaced by academic projections. Asked on the BBC radio programme *Desert Island Discs* in 2020 about the motivation behind her pioneering depiction of multi-racial characters in her books, the celebrated illustrator Helen Oxenbury replied that she simply draws the world that she sees around her.

Illustration is also an activity that has spawned an industry of self-learning leisure-pursuit products; books, correspondence courses and more recently video downloads. With the enduring perception of illustration as a hybrid subject, straddling fine art and graphic design, the activity tended throughout much of the twentieth century to emerge from one or other of these two study routes, both of which were firmly based in the formal teaching of drawing. In the UK and US, from the 1970s onwards, discrete, named undergraduate and postgraduate courses in illustration began to appear. It remains the

case that aspiring illustrators are taught primarily by established practitioners, and the need to guide and nurture their development based on individual creative leanings and directions is still paramount. As the illustrator and educator John Vernon Lord observes in *Drawing Upon Drawing* (University of Brighton, 2007):

> It is important to build up a relationship with students, one in which there is mutual trust and understanding. Timing is of the essence – recognizing promising directions in students' work at precisely the right moment...and encouraging them to develop something along these lines and go all out for it.

While emphasizing that good illustration is about much more than drawing, Lord goes on to suggest:

> One of the best antidotes to overcoming problems in your work as an illustrator, I think, is to draw from direct observation. Trying to make visual sense of what you can see in front of you, and translating

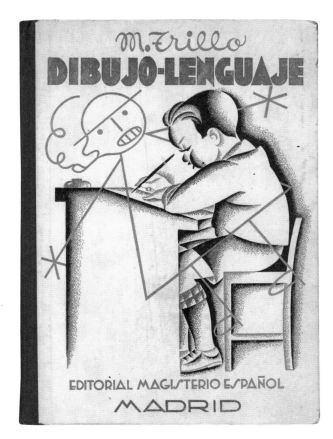

this by making an image on a flat surface,
is always an overwhelming challenge –
well worth taking on if you are at a low
ebb with your work.

From a teaching perspective, the relationship between drawing, illustration, generalizable knowledge and the needs of the individual artist have always been a matter for debate and dispute, as illustrated by the following two mid-twentieth century British illustrators Edward Ardizzone and Lynton Lamb.

OPPOSITE AND ABOVE: Throughout the twentieth century many leading commercial artists were commissioned to pass on their knowledge in popular 'how-to' books. Shown here are leading poster designer Gregory Brown's *How to Draw Trees* (The Studio, 1943); *Art School For Everyone – Everywhere*, published by Albert Dorne and Norman Rockwell's Famous Artists School correspondence course in 1962; volume 6 of *¡ya dibujo!*, Andrés Sepúlveda's drawing manuals; and Manuel Trillo's *Dibujo-Lenguage*, first published in 1935.

'It seems that (Ardizzone) keeps his nose to the paper and draws out of his head. When he makes his characters turn a leg or drop a curtsey, they do it so well because he has always copied the very best masters'

Edward Ardizzone and Lynton Lamb 'Born' or 'true'?

There are two things that all born illustrators have in common. The first is that their creative imagination is fired by the written word rather than the thing seen; the second is that when it comes to their illustrations, they would rather make them up than have recourse to life. In fact, as a rule, they don't like drawing from life at all.

So wrote one of the greatest illustrators of the twentieth century, Edward Ardizzone, in 1957, having been persuaded to write a rare, short essay expounding his views on the key qualities that make a good illustrator. The following year, he gave an address at a meeting of the Double Crown Club in Brighton, England, in which he recycled his views under the title 'The Born Illustrator'. His speech was published in the first issue of the graphic arts journal Motif in November of that year. Ardizzone's views, expressed in a somewhat dogmatic manner, caused

considerable controversy. They were, he said, partly informed by his role as a visiting teacher of Illustration at the Royal College of Art. He was dismissive of much illustration of the time and, most surprisingly, of the importance of direct observational drawing in the development of the illustrator, citing the illustrators George Cruikshank and Honoré-Victorin Daumier as examples to back up his argument: 'One denied that he ever drew from life and the other was never seen to do so'.

Ardizzone's point that the born illustrator prefers to create 'his own version of the world around him' was, and of course still is, to some extent true. But Ardizzone, while not having had a formal art school education, had attended a rigorous programme of life drawing and painting under the tuition of the figurative painter Bernard Meninsky, which he mentions only in passing. He doesn't

seem to differentiate between drawing from life as sight-skill-building and drawing from life as illustration reference. He asserts that most illustration students would do better if they learned by copying from the work of the great masters and then by 'drawing a thing over and over again until it looks right'. This, he continues, is how the born illustrator gradually compiles a sort of 'dictionary of forms', helped by instructional books on such subjects as 'how to draw trees'. He only somewhat grudgingly advises that it can be useful to occasionally return to direct observation from the nature to 'confirm' or 'sweeten' knowledge.

This should, of course, be seen in the context of the time in which it was written. Ardizzone was endeavouring to contrast the painter's need for embedded academic drawing skills with the illustrator's narrative imagination. Perhaps he was trying to make

Above: Edward Ardizzone developed specific working methods that he claimed were not primarily rooted in direct observational drawing, but in 'finding a way to draw things'. His strong sense of light and shade was executed through his distinctive pen and ink cross-hatching technique. This was usually preceded by careful planning in soft pencil, as shown in this illustration from *Brief to Counsel* by Henry Cecil (Michael Joseph, 1958).

Edward Ardizzone and Lynton Lamb

Drawing and Illustration

Opposite and above: Ardizzone revered the work of the great Victorian illustrator
George Cruikshank. He felt that Cruikshank's illustration of Charles Dickens's Fagin
in his condemned cell, shown here in final engraved form alongside a sheet of
preparatory studies, was one of the great examples of dramatic illustration.

Edward Ardizzone and Lynton Lamb

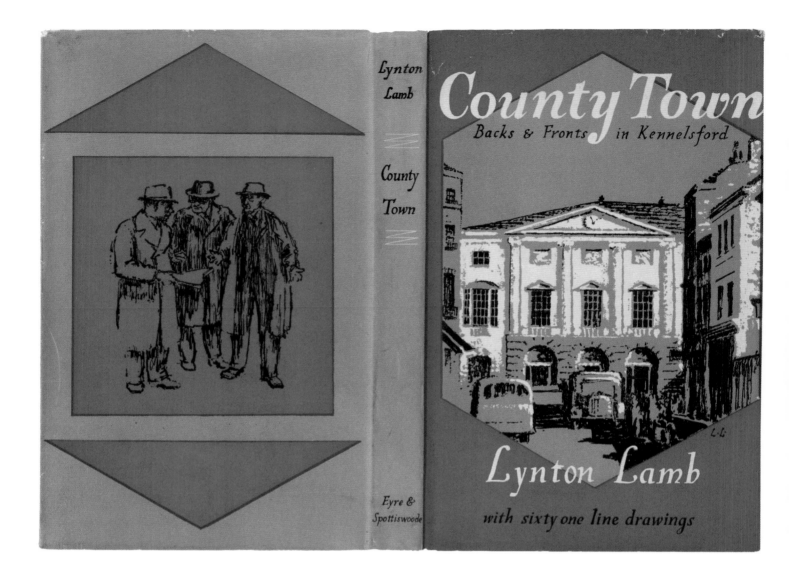

clear that being a great draughtsman is not the primary qualification for good illustration, but in doing so he appears to suggest that observational drawing skills could be a hindrance to the illustrator's imagination. Such a view must also have been influenced by his own particular, unusual genius in observing human, social behaviour with an acute visual memory. In his biography of Ardizzone, his brother-in-law Gabriel White recalls seeing the artist sitting on a park bench, drawing in his sketchbook a scene from memory while simultaneously observing and committing to memory a group of nearby characters.

The second issue of *Motif* was published in February 1959. In it, Lynton Lamb, a very different kind of illustrator, took Ardizzone to task under the title 'The True Illustrator', opening with more than a hint of sarcasm:

In Motif No.1, Edward Ardizzone explained how he works as an illustrator. It seems that he keeps his nose to the paper and draws out of his head. When he makes his characters turn a leg or drop a curtsey, they do it so well because he has always copied the very best masters. However, he likes to take a peek at life from time to time to see if it is conforming to precept. If it is not, it is probably out of character.

Lamb explains that he does not work out of his head but from copious notes and references. He was a painter as well as an illustrator, and his work was rigidly rooted in observation. There is no hint of the playfulness and warmth that characterized Ardizzone's drawings, as he explains:

I work standing at a high bench; and however small the scale of my illustration may be or however closely knit to its typographic setting, I always check the 'colour values' of its tonal pattern and its final balance and tension, by looking at it from a painting distance on my easel.

Lamb, if rather dryly, argues that there are many valid approaches to the relationship between drawing from nature and drawing for illustration. He concedes that, in the words of the seventeenth-century century dramatist Richard Flecknoe, 'Truth hath no greater enemy than verisimilitude or likelihood'. Ultimately, he concludes, 'the important thing is the transmutation of artifice or fact to a moment of dramatic truth'.

For many working illustrators today, even the opportunity to, as Ardizzone put it, occasionally 'sweeten' from life can be elusive. But the building blocks will nevertheless be in place to provide a lifelong underpinning.

Opposite: Lynton Lamb's illustration work was informed by a formal art education as a painter. He wrote and illustrated *County Town*, based on everyday life in his home town of Chelmsford (Eyre & Spottiswoode, 1950). Above: A rare surviving wartime copy of *Parade* magazine, featuring an early Edward Ardizzone cover design with fully hand-drawn imagery and lettering.

Edward Ardizzone and Lynton Lamb

CHAPTER 2

The Basics

Learning to see

'Once one has drawn from observation a
bicycle, its workings and construction are
forever ingrained in memory. We *know*
a bicycle in a completely different way'

The 'mechanics' of drawing can be variously broken down into constituent parts. For the beginner, it would be extremely difficult (and probably counterproductive) to try to consciously juggle all of these elements while drawing; line, tone, composition and so on are often employed unconsciously, and eventually form an integrated whole. They are learned primarily through drawing and through looking at drawings.

It is a common misconception that an ability to draw is an innate 'gift' that individuals either are or are not in possession of. It is also often assumed that drawing is primarily a hand skill. While, as with many other activities, some people will develop a particular affinity with or ability to express themselves through drawing, the basics of learning to draw what you see can be learned by most. First, it is necessary to understand what 'seeing' actually means. A useful way of demonstrating this is through what has long been a standard project in the first weeks of study on an undergraduate illustration course, and which can be undertaken by anyone in their own time. Take a list of ten things that you are bound to have 'seen' within the previous twenty-four hours. Some of these will depend on the locale in which the project takes place, but they might include, for example, a bicycle, the main entrance to the institution, a bank note or coin, a prominent monument in the city centre. Then, make a drawing from memory of each of these on a single large sheet of paper, with plenty of space between each. Once this is completed, go out and draw each of the items directly from observation alongside your memory drawings.

The results are always revelatory – invariably demonstrating how little of our visible world we genuinely *see*. Once one has drawn from observation a bicycle, its workings and construction are forever ingrained in memory. We *know* a bicycle in a completely different way. This project provides an important lesson in how to begin to distrust those insistent messages from the brain, trying to tell us that we *know*, as it does battle with our

---

The Basics

eyes, which are trying to lead us to a different kind of knowing – visual knowing. No tricks or clever techniques can replace this kind of knowledge.

'Blind drawing' is a useful way of continuing to build knowledge of the visual world. The term refers to drawing while keeping the eyes permanently focused on the subject of the drawing and not allowing oneself to look at the drawing itself as it evolves. This of course means that the drawing may not 'join up' at all and involves a complete lack of control over any perceived ideas of 'finish'. But it enforces total dependence on the eyes at the expense of any retreat into a preconceived 'safe zone' of generalized rendering. It is, of course, a means to an end, the end being the gradual building of visual understanding.

In any event, when drawing from observation, it is advisable to aim to spend something like seventy per cent of the time with eyes focused on the subject and a maximum of thirty per cent with eyes focused on the paper. This is the reverse ratio of what tends to happen instinctively, so it requires considerable discipline and focus (I have often joked with students that I intend to patent a drawing aid in the form of a neck brace that locks the head into a position that only allows its wearer to look forwards, but has a timed release mechanism to allow periodic short glances at the sketchbook). The more you do this the more natural it becomes. In time, this kind of looking becomes habitual, increasingly leading to a habit of 'mentally drawing' when not actually physically drawing. You will find yourself looking at, for example, a figure on a park bench and registering the line of the shoulders through the head or the tension in the folds of a coat created by the bend of an elbow.

The Basics

way of the sheep

little market monday 8th February

Tools and materials

'Discovering whether one is ultimately most comfortable drawing expansively with a twig dipped in ink or intimately with a 7H pencil takes time and artistic self-knowledge'

The wide range of materials and drawing tools that are available to artists today can be highly seductive. There is always a temptation to believe that this or that tool will lead to a better drawing. While experimenting with a range of media is ultimately important, when trying to get to grips with the basics of drawing, it is advisable to focus on the process of learning to see rather than giving in to the distractions of the respective effects that can be created by the myriad drawing implements available. A humble 3B or 4B pencil is difficult to better in terms of the range of linear and tonal marks that it can deliver, especially when drawing on location with the need to get visual information down on paper at speed. Once confidence in drawing begins to grow, many will branch out to explore and experiment before ultimately finding the tools and media that best suit their own artistic temperament. Discovering whether one is ultimately most comfortable drawing expansively with a twig dipped in ink or intimately with a 7H pencil takes time and artistic self-knowledge. Of course, the tools that you use will have a bearing on the scale at which you work, and it is surprising how often this can be overlooked. Trying to draw at a large scale with a hard pencil or delicate nib can be as dispiriting as using a lump of charcoal in a tiny sketchbook.

When it comes to making illustration, the wide choice of media, traditional and digital, becomes much more relevant and is touched on further through the work of many artists throughout this book.

OPPOSITE: One of greatest illustrators of his time, Ronald Searle always remained almost reverential in his respect for his tools. As well as numerous trial sheets, he kept a framed collection of nibs (bottom left), each labelled and written with the nib being described.

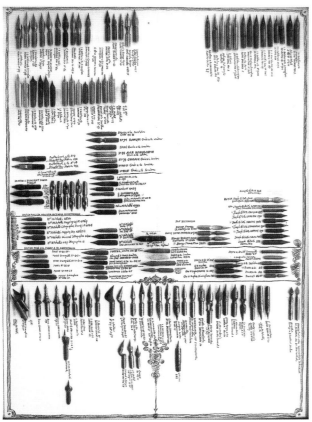

Tools and materials

Line

'The line as a tool for describing and
commenting visually is still fundamental
to drawing for illustration'

In Chapter 1, we touched on the huge leap of faith that is involved in accepting the convention of an outline as a representation of form, an ability that, as far as we know, only humans possess. And even for us, it has to be learned. But the drawn line, more than the outlines of shapes, can express rhythm, movement, light, space and much more, as the artist grows an understanding of its handling and potential.

The typographer and book designer Douglas Martin perfectly expressed the concept of the illustrator's use of line as a 'voice' in titling his 1989 collection of essays on leading book illustrators *The Telling Line*. It is a phrase that still resonates, even though it could be argued that today's illustrators may be slightly less dependent on line than those whose careers were forged mainly at a time when black and white letterpress line-block printing predominated. The line as a tool for describing and commenting visually is still fundamental to drawing for illustration, with its ability, in the right hands, to express so much more than the boundaries of shapes.

OPPOSITE: Egon Schiele's mastery of the expressive potential of the drawn line is perfectly captured in this 1914 drawing of Friederike Maria Beer, *Woman with Arms Raised*.
FOLLOWING SPREAD: Until the 1960s, a great deal of black and white line illustration was still printed using the letterpress line block. Process White opaque gouache was used to paint over 'mistakes', as can be seen in this original artwork by Susan Einzig from *The Children's Song Book* (text by Elizabeth Poston, The Bodley Head, 1961).

The Basics

Skip, Skip, Skip to my Lou.

The Basics

Skip, skip, skip to my Lou,
Skip, skip, skip to my Lou,
Skip, skip, skip to my Lou,
  Skip to my Lou, my darling.

Partner's gone, what will I do?
Partner's gone, what will I do?
Partner's gone, what will I do?
  Skip to my Lou, my darling.

Skip, skip, &c.

Tone

'Plot the areas of light against
dark until the shape of the subject
begins to emerge from the gloom'

As we have seen, illustrators have traditionally tended to think in terms of line to describe where shapes begin and end and to tell stories. But some subject matter demands tonal treatment, typically where strong lighting and atmosphere are key to the subject's representation. Working tonally from observation means thinking in a completely different way. Learning to see and describe form and volume through the fall of light on three-dimensional shapes can be facilitated by abandoning the idea of making dark marks on a light surface.

An excellent way to start is by covering a sheet of paper with soft graphite or charcoal and rubbing in to make a mid-tone. Then, instead of drawing with a pencil or charcoal, 'draw' with an eraser.

Plot the areas of light against dark until the shape of the subject begins to emerge from the gloom. Once again, this means spending much more time looking at the subject than at the drawing. When engaged in a tonal drawing such as this, I invariably find myself screwing up my eyes until they are almost closed, in order to clear away all of the distracting detail so that I can measure the relative tones of one surface against another. It helps to disentangle 'local' colour (i.e. the actual colour of surfaces – a dark blue wall or a brown desk) from the relative strength of tones. A white-painted wall in deep shadow can be darker than a blue wall in strong sunlight. Time to drown out the noise of the brain and 'listen' to the eyes again.

OPPOSITE: In this drawing by Pam Smy, made as an undergraduate illustration student, her primary concern was to establish the relative tonal values in a challenging scene where the tonal range was extremely narrow. Only the few areas of pure light are left unshaded, brought back with the use of an eraser to reveal the white of the paper.

FOLLOWING SPREAD: A good way to develop an understanding of tone is to draw at night. In this sketchbook image of a railway station exterior, Seoungjun Baek cleverly simplifies a complex scene, picking out the light sources and the fall of diluted light on surfaces using charcoal, eraser and white ink pen.

The Basics

OPPOSITE AND ABOVE: Making fully tonal drawings in the life-drawing studio to describe space, this unnamed student at the Cambridge School of Art rubbed down a layer of charcoal into the paper and 'drew' the fall of light with the eraser, gradually re-establishing darker darks and adding minimal line here and there to clarify some boundaries. The shapes around the figure are as important to its description as the figure itself.

Using line to describe tone

'Artists...developed various
ingenious ways of mark-making
in solid "line" in order to create
the illusion of continuous tone'

For much of its history, the appearance of illustration has been closely linked to the requirements and limitations of commercial printing processes. In the past, reproduction of continuous tonal gradation from artwork, created using media such as pencil or washes, was much more expensive than that which had been executed in solid blacks. Printers' use of half-tone screens to photographically convert continuous tonal washes into tiny black dots of varying size and density could lead to rather insipid results. The word 'line' was applied, perhaps a little misleadingly, to the production of original artwork using only solid blacks (i.e. no washes or pencil work containing tonal gradation). Artists therefore developed various ingenious ways of mark-making in solid black 'line' in order to create the illusion of continuous tone. These included cross-hatching, stippling and the use of 'mechanical tints' – commercially produced, pre-printed sheets of dots and lines that could be cut out and stuck down onto the artwork. The differences in printing costs are now minimal, but the descriptive and decorative effects that these originally purely functional processes and approaches give remain popular.

OPPOSITE ABOVE: Eric Hobbs collaged a range of mechanical tints to create this 'line' printed illustration, used to explain the workings of an advertising agency in *Drawing for Advertising* (The Studio, 1956).

OPPOSITE BELOW: In this drawing made on the Croatian island of Šipan, I was concerned to show the contrast between the dark tones and textures of the scrub-covered hillside across the bay, and the light falling on the sea. This meant building up a sense of continuous tone with a lot of line-work.

Using line to describe tone

Mark-making and printmaking

'Gestural mark-making can be a way
of expressing a more emotional
or tactile response to your subject'

In its broadest sense, the term 'mark-making' refers to the many and varied forms of mark that can be produced with different implements on a variety of surfaces. It tends to be more specifically associated with the kind of drawing that employs dynamic and perhaps experimental or intuitive approaches to drawing through expressive exploration of lines, shapes and textures. As well as the direct making of marks on a surface, this can include scratching into layers of ink or pastel to create marks and shapes by revealing the surface below. Gestural mark-making can be a way of expressing a more emotional or tactile response to your subject, whether from direct observation or from memory or imagination. It inevitably means giving in to a degree of loss of control and embracing accident.

Mark-making in drawing naturally overlaps with and includes the use of 'print'. By 'print', I mean the application of inks or other liquid media to an object or surface before pressing it onto paper or another surface to leave a (reverse) trans-ferred impression. This is where the boundaries between drawing and printmaking become blurred. Printmaking itself can often be an activity rooted in drawing for limited editions of reproduction, while drawing directly onto paper may incorporate elements of print.

In Chapter 1 I observed how, in Lynton Lamb's 1962 *Drawing for Illustration*, a great deal of attention was inevitably given to the need for illustrators to use methods, tools and materials that would best allow their work to reproduce well through the print processes of the day, including the preparation of colour separations for letter-press printing. Although there is still a need to give some thought to what kind of approaches will reproduce best on paper or screen, advances in technology have made such issues somewhat less critical. Paradoxically, however, interest in traditional printmaking processes for the 'raw' or organic aesthetic that they can facilitate has grown. Often these processes are combined with digital ones as a means of assemblage. Some printmaking processes, such as etching and lithography, can involve drawing directly onto the plate or stone. Others, such as screenprinting and linocut, tend to involve the need to think in terms of shape rather than line.

OPPOSITE: In this location drawing by Anna Ring, a range of marks are employed, using inks and coloured pencils to contrast loose fine lines with vigorously applied areas of tone and pattern.

TOP: Nastya Smirnova's *Self-portrait, Cambodia* uses stippling and repeat printing of shapes to create a vibrant example of mark-making.

ABOVE: In this image, Hye-Young Kim's highly personal and expressive approach to drawing features delicate, sensitive mark-making with broadly applied washes of colour.

OPPOSITE: Combining painted textures and collage with monoprint drawing, Hanieh Ghashghaei successfully integrates a range of marks into a unified whole.

Christopher Brown
Drawing for linocut

Christopher Brown's highly respected work as an illustrator and teacher spans the decades since he completed his studies at London's Royal College of Art in the 1970s. Through the college, he was introduced to Edward Bawden, one of the most important figures in the history of the linocut and the whole of the graphic arts. On graduating, Brown's work soon became a familiar sight in the stylish magazines and design publications of the time. Over the years he has become increasingly associated with linocut, and works both to commission and for himself. In 2012 he created his illustrated *An Alphabet of London*, each spread of which presents visually a place or aspect of his home city in a playfully cryptic manner, with little implied narratives interwoven into the pages. Born and raised in Putney, he wanted to reflect his love of the city and its many faces. Here, he muses on the sometimes complex and more specific relationship between drawing and design for him, and in the context of his chosen medium.

I've never really considered myself a draughtsman. While at the RCA I was in awe of those who could effortlessly record what was in front of them. During the first and second years (of what was then a three-year course) my illustrations were based on life filtered through my imagination; it was only when I went to stay at the college's Paris studio that I really started to draw what was around me. It was my tutor Sheila Robinson who sent me off to meet Edward Bawden, and it was on our subsequent sketching holidays to Cornwall that I learned how to draw – from observing Edward and persevering. I tried to put into practice what I learned on those holidays with EB when it came to the Alphabet.

In my bag I always try to have a sketchbook, a small Moleskine notebook (I prefer the paper to that of the sketchbook) and a Fineliner pen (0.3). When it comes to drawing for a project I use three methods – drawing from memory or what I imagine, drawing from reference from found images and, finally, drawing from observation. An Alphabet of London incorporated all three methods, but it was the third that was the most important – I had to visit all of the locations from A to Z – from 'Queen Anne's Alcove' to the 'Zoo'.

The drawing was vital for me to design the cut – it had to work for the square format I had (perhaps unwisely) chosen. The sketches are to help me design the final image. They are an aide mémoire – and really for my eyes only – I would feel rather ashamed to show them to a topographical artist! These sketches are important for me to get a sense of place – the time of day, the people walking and, of course, any dogs.

Edward always advised me when sketching to try and be in a position where people don't look over your shoulder – most off-putting! My sketches are quick, so perhaps the unwelcome viewer doesn't have time to catch me.

I also learned from Edward to try different points of view – what makes the best 'design'. It's not about verisimilitude, it's about trying to make an interesting composition that can then be refined when back at the studio. A lamp post or pillar box may be moved or even added. And certainly populating an image with characters that might well have been seen but equally might be imagined. In 'W is for Westminster',

Above, following spread and pp. 74–75: The drawings that Christopher Brown makes for his linocuts primarily take the form of compositional plans that are ultimately executed in the form of flat shapes. The initial outline drawings are transferred onto the lino blocks using tracing paper. The blocks are then ready for cutting.

Christopher Brown

the nun and the chap on the mobile were observed and the monsignor was added partly because I wanted a figure to balance the composition, but also because I wanted a splash of red in the picture. In 'Y is for York Hall' I thought it would be amusing to have a towelled, plump, pink figure, as if he had come from the Turkish baths.

Colour is also important. I note the colour on location and will take a photo as a reminder, but the colour is added to reinforce the design – if I was to be true to colours on the days on which I sketched the place the pages would have had a very similar palette. Skies can be yellow, pink or purple if I so wish.

Once back in the studio I will transfer my sketch onto layout paper and draw and redraw the design until it feels correct. The areas of colour are blocked in using Pantones, so that when it comes to mixing colours I can hopefully replicate. The Alphabet was produced in a relatively short period of time, about six months, and much as I would have liked to produce twenty-six full-colour prints I just didn't have the time, so I printed up blocks of textures that could be scanned and laid down using Photoshop.

The obvious difference between my sketch and the final cut is the weight of line. My drawings are rather fine and scribbly, the

cuts far bolder and more graphic. Although, as I said, drawing is not what I consider my strength, it is vital to my working process. When I was with Edward Bawden in Cornwall the drawing was a more relaxed process, Edward working on two paintings a day, I labouring away with my pencils – I really should have picked up brush and watercolour like Edward! I still have some of his initial sketches drawn in 2B that he discarded. It's interesting to see how loose those first marks of his are, quickly working out a composition before applying colour.

The Basics

Christopher Brown

The Basics

Christopher Brown

Composition and structure

'As you gain confidence in drawing,
identifying and incorporating an overall
sense of structure becomes more possible'

'Composition' is really another word for 'arrangement'. Whether applied to the positioning of a single object within a given space or the arrangement of a complex assembly of elements into a harmonious whole, it is a fundamental aspect of drawing. When we encounter a visual image for the first time, a considerable proportion of our response to that image is registered in the first millisecond of seeing it. We respond to its basic structure and dynamics, the 'building blocks', well before we have registered any of the pictorial narrative detail contained within it. It is therefore essential to develop a strong sense of composition in planning an image through drawing. It can be very easy when preoccupied with rendering detail to lose track of the underlying arrangement of shapes and the dialogue between them. This becomes particularly important in the context of drawing for picturebook illustration, where the artist not only has to consider shapes in relation to a single frame or page, but also in relation to the central vertical gutter of a double-page spread. On top of this, the positioning of the lines of text must be considered from the outset as part of the overall design concept of the page. One of the things that I find myself saying more

often than any other when working with children's book-illustration students on picturebook-making is 'if your image is perfectly composed *before* you have added the text, it's a bad composition'.

When drawing scenes of daily life directly from observation, especially when the subject involves people on the move, retaining a sense of composition can be particularly challenging. Getting the basic 'architecture' of the space satisfactorily positioned at the outset allows for flexibility of content within the overall structure, letting moving elements enter and leave the field of vision. It is advisable not to be too preoccupied by composition when learning to draw from observation; trying to juggle too many things at this stage can be counterproductive and dispiriting. But as you gain confidence in drawing, identifying and incorporating an overall sense of structure becomes more possible. To this end, knowing what to leave out becomes at least as important as knowing what to include when drawing.

As an artist, you are not a camera. Drawing a scene from observation involves a great deal of decision-making about what to include, where to position yourself, how to frame the image, what

OPPOSITE: Paul Hogarth was a master of dynamic composition in his reportage drawings. In this 1963 drawing of the Pratt, Read & Co. Road piano-key factory in the Connecticut River Valley, he renders the intricate brickwork to create a dynamic dialogue between line and textured tone. Reproduced in *Paul Hogarth's American Album* (Lion & Unicorn Press, 1973).

The Basics

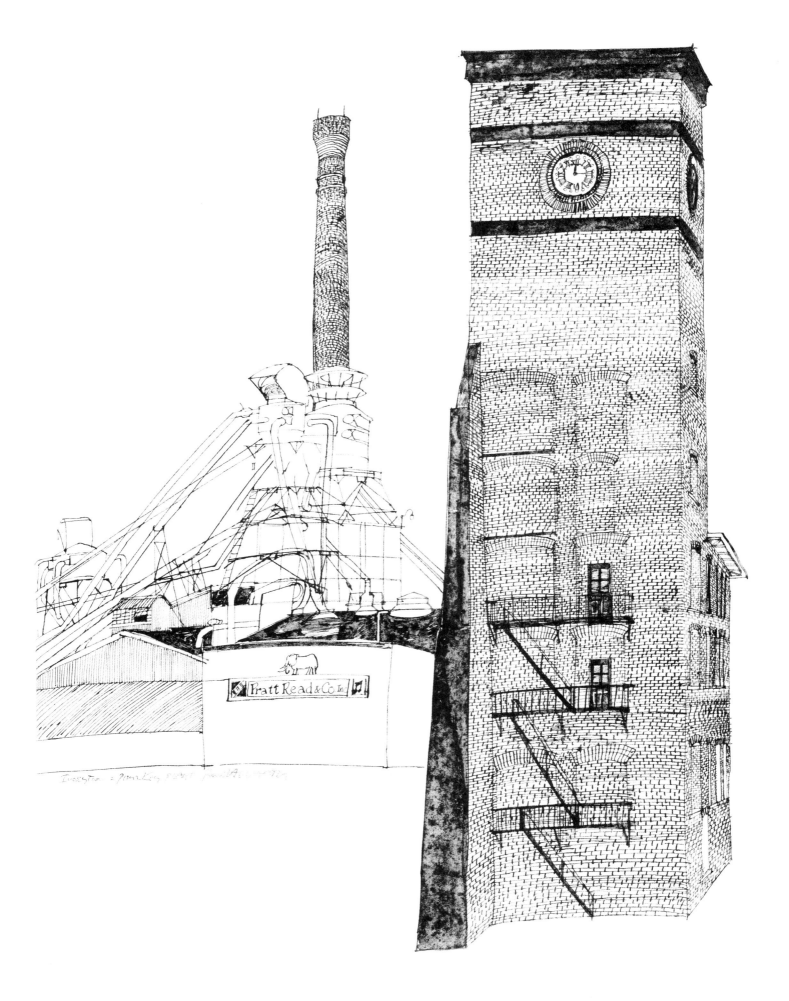

Ivoryton + Dann River Street, Pratt Read & Co...

overall shape of image best suits the subject. So often one will see a student begin a drawing in the centre of a sketchbook page and end it when the drawing 'falls off the edge' of it. The shape of the sketchbook page may not be the best shape for your subject, so it is important to not allow it to dictate to you. Either choose a composition that works best within the shape of the page or spread, or make a frame within it that is best for your concept.

As with many areas of the arts, throughout history there have been many mathematical formulae applied to compositional structures in art, perhaps most notably the identification of the 'Golden Section' or 'Mean' by the fifteenth-century Italian mathematician Luca Pacioli. Put simply,

his proposition was that when, in linear terms, the short piece is to the long piece as the long piece is to the whole, an aesthetically satisfying, perfectly balanced composition is achieved. Although it can be helpful to play around with this formula on paper to gain a full understanding of its meaning and application, it is debatable how much conscious use can be derived from it when actually drawing. As the illustrator, curator, painter and writer Barbara Jones put it so eloquently in her typically no-nonsense instructional book, *Water-colour Painting: A Practical Guide* (Adam and Charles Black, 1960): '*Alas, it is a fact that although almost every good painting can be turned into mathematics, it is almost impossible to start with the mathematics and get a good painting.*'

ABOVE: A ceramicist as well as illustrator, Aude Van Ryn uses colour as a compositional tool to divide space and draw the eye to the figure in this drawing, which was made on location at London's Kew Gardens.

OPPOSITE: Barbara Jones used a no-nonsense approach to explain issues of composition in her 1960 book *Water-colour Painting*. These very rough, quick sketches describe perfectly, with wry humour, some of the 'dos and don'ts'.

The Basics

Plain white paper; perfect. Why touch it? If you must, consider the following academic crimes before you start:

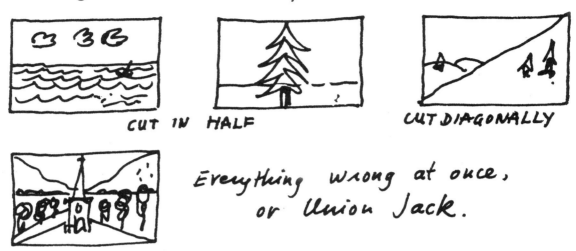

In landscape painting it is common to balance an enormous mass with a bright or dark speck; Corot was very keen on this trick,

Perspective

'It is not necessary to study all of
the complex rules of perspective
in order to grasp the basics'

Formal rules of perspective are rarely taught these days outside the context of architectural or technical drawing. But, as with all rules, a broad understanding of the principles is useful, whether the artist ultimately chooses to adhere to or consciously flout them. There are various strands to the history of the use of formal linear perspective in art, and some debate about its origins. Filippo Brunelleschi is generally credited with being the 'reinventor' of the system of converging parallel lines to describe the illusion of receding space on a flat surface. Wall paintings from as far back as the first century BC, found near Pompeii, contain some examples of single-point perspective, but not in a manner that suggests a fully evolved mathematical approach. In East Asia, a much softer approach was generally used to convey distance, using layers of gently receding banks of tone in both painting and printmaking.

It is not necessary to study all of the complex rules of perspective in order to grasp the basics. Much can be acquired through the process of drawing from observation: a simple awareness of eye-level and the use of a pencil held up horizontally against, for example, a distant rooftop to establish its angle. There have been many instructional books on the subject of perspective published over the years. One of the cleverest is Gwen White's 1954 *A Book of Pictorial Perspective* (John Murray, 1954), with illustrations drawn directly on the lithographic plate by the author. It ingeniously allows the reader to see technical perspective diagrams overlaid onto each of the three-colour illustrations. This was achieved by printing linear diagrams of the colour scenes on the reverse side of the paper, each one 'flipped' or reversed so that it lines up exactly with the colour image when held up to the light.

One of the most useful and commonly encouraged exercises to understand the principles of perspective is to look through a window on to a scene outside, ideally including straight-edged structures, such as buildings. Try to imagine that the scene is not a scene at all but a painting on the glass, the window frame being the frame of a two-dimensional painting or drawing. Close one eye and imagine that you are drawing or 'tracing' the lines of the buildings directly onto the glass with a very long pencil. The frame of the window forms a picture frame and helps clarify the angles of the shapes.

OPPOSITE: Gwen White's ingenious method of teaching perspective involved holding the pages of a book up to the light in order to reveal the instructional lines laid over the colour image. Here, we have flipped the colour image in order to see them together.

FOLLOWING SPREAD: I made this drawing over a period of two to three hours in the garden of an old house on the Croatian island of Šipan. The portico-style structure gave a natural drama of receding perspective. My eye-level was about a third of the way up the composition.

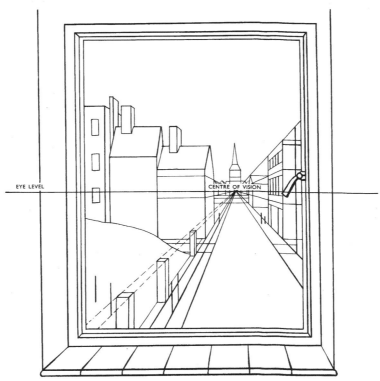

Perspective

Lélo's garden

Drawing
and colour

'The human eye can distinguish
between somewhere in the region
of a million colours'

We tend to think of drawing in terms of black and white and painting in terms of colour. But there are various intermediary forms where colour is used in drawing. At what point a coloured drawing becomes a painting is something of a moot point, but a painting is usually conceived at the outset as such, even though drawing will sometimes play a role in its planning and development. Using colour in observational drawing can take many forms. Inevitably, this involves a great deal more 'juggling' and constant decision-making with regards to how far to go, what to include and what to leave out in order to retain some control of the overall design. Using a predetermined limited palette can be a useful 'way in' to working with

colour, beginning with just two complementary colours, one warm and one cool. As with any other aspect of learning to draw, learning to see and *think* in terms of colour is crucial. Many illustration students (including myself many years ago) struggle with colour. Others are fortunate enough to have a seemingly effortless and intuitive flair for its use. It's a complex subject, but always remember that it is generally understood that the human eye can distinguish between somewhere in the region of a million colours, so the twelve or so that you have in your bag or pencil case are not going to magically be the ones that you need. They are a starting point for a great deal of careful mixing in order to achieve exactly what you want.

OPPOSITE: A very quick line and wash sketch made at my allotment. White inks were used last of all, to pick out light against dark and add texture to the drawing.
FOLLOWING SPREAD: This spectacular coloured pen and

wash drawing by Olga Shevchenko does not attempt to describe space and depth, but revels in contrasts of scale and the delicate dialogue between lines, shapes and surface texture.

The Basics

'I'm conscious that the white space of the paper plays a big role in the composition and harmony of the piece'

Vyara Boyadjieva
Line, form, colour

Vyara Boyadjieva is an artist and picturebook-maker from Bulgaria. Her work is rooted in observational skills that underpin a highly imaginative, subjective illustrative language. She often creates her illustrations in paint, working in a fully tonal idiom, representing space and depth through receding tones and colours. Here, she reflects on some of these aspects in her work.

I merge forms and lines by intuition, I think. What I mean by intuition is that these decisions don't always have a rational explanation, but rather are guided by the impression of the place, the momentary experience and inevitably one's personal state. While sketching, I always strive to create visual harmony, so I constantly check and if I can't find it, I correct it by balancing with lines, forms and colour. Concretely, I try to refine areas of the sketch that are either too full or too empty, bearing in mind the form/line relation.

What I always ask myself when painting is 'are these colours fighting for attention, or are they serving each other for the sake of the whole?' You can have chromatic harmony only when some of them, with their presence, are making others look more beautiful. This is something that I apply to the line and form dynamic, too. There are cases where form is too ponderous and steals the stage without necessarily conveying anything, and other cases where the line is too quiet and lacks vibrancy, and we can barely hear what it wants to tell us! So I'd say that I can't follow a recipe, but I make sure to always have my 'harmony' radar on. The colour palette evolves as I work! I already have a limited choice of coloured pencils, and I know that once I've started with some, I won't be using others, as they don't match together. But this selection always happens consequently and naturally.

I'm conscious that the white space of the paper plays a big role in the composition and harmony of the piece and it's a very useful tool to narrate as well. I think I use it more wisely when I sketch with just lines (ink pen), as I feel I'm only equipped with the lines and the white to tell something. I really enjoy playing with this big entity that is the white paper in a duet with the thin black line of the ink pen. Strangely, I'm not that sensitive about it when I'm using colour. Maybe because I rely too much on the narration that other colours bring, and the white colour of the paper comes more as an extra than a protagonist. It can be used as a negative space, but I rarely do it, and I must confess that I often undervalue its potential in my colour sketch work.

Usually when I paint, I think of all the elements in terms of forms, instead of lines. But when I sketch, the circumstances and the objective are very different. In order to get as much information as you would like, you need to be fast, as life in front of you is moving and changing continually. I try to adapt my thinking to the circumstances on the street, which are uncontrollable and untamed and inspire me to lose control when transferring them onto paper. This is where the line drawing comes in handy, because it describes and tells without slowing you down; it's more spontaneous in a way.

I love colour, but even if I use it with line only, it still demands decisions in terms of colour combinations, when a 'simple' black line doesn't. And thus the black line gives you a chance to be fully immersed in the observation. So I'd say colour sketches are to me sometimes irrelevant if colour is not needed to narrate or portray a feeling. I think it makes you clumsy and slow in a fast-moving situation that you could only catch with quick moves of the ink pen that follow the slightest motions of your hand. The results often look more vulnerable and shakier, because I've spent more time staring at the object than looking at the paper.

The Basics

Above: Vyara Boyadjieva's colour-pencil drawings are rooted in direct observation, but do not aim for pure realism. The drawings combine direct observation with intuitive pattern-making and design.

Vyara Boyadjieva

People and environments

'Developing a healthy combination of
detached analysis of shape and subjective
interest in movement and interaction is key'

Very few illustrators' bodies of work have developed successfully without an interest in drawing people. Of course, there are many successful graphic artists whose work is driven more by an interest in, for example, surface pattern and design, but bearing in mind that the vast majority of subject matter for illustration emerges from the human experience, relationships and storytelling of one sort or another, even in the field of non-fiction, the representation of the human figure would seem to be of paramount importance. Formal study in the life room of the naked figure has been central to the education of generations of art students. Understanding the human form through such analytical drawing has been seen as the foundation for all forms of visual art throughout most of the history of art education. It is probably fair to say that fewer and fewer establishments still exist where such teaching still takes place.

The views expressed respectively by Edward Ardizzone and Lynton Lamb give us insights into the complex issues around 'academic' drawing and 'anecdotal' drawing. By 'anecdotal' drawing, I mean drawing that is motivated primarily by subjective interest in human behaviour and interaction, as distinct from a primarily academic interest in form and structure. Certainly such intense interest is clear to see in all of Edward Ardizzone's illustrative work, while another of the great twentieth-century illustrators, Ronald Searle, when asked what he would have been had he not been an illustrator, is said to have replied 'a voyeur'.

Drawing people is of course more difficult than drawing static subjects. Not just because they are always on the move, but also due to the fact that we spend so much time looking at them, in everyday life and also on screens, that our minds are filled with preconceptions about what they look like. So developing a healthy combination of detached analysis of shape and subjective interest in movement and interaction is key. Another factor that can inhibit students when drawing people is the fear of their subjects becoming aware that they are being drawn. So it is important to develop strategies to enable the artist to feel comfortable and able to fully focus on the job at hand. When drawing in places where people congregate, such as markets and shopping malls, I often recommend seeking out viewpoints from above. People rarely look up, so it is possible to study their natural movements and gestures

OPPOSITE: Charlotte Bownass was fortunate enough to have access to this RADA scenic art workshop in 2012. She made the most of the opportunity to explore people in relation to their very specific environment, using the full height and width of the open sketchbook to express the relative scale of figures and interior space.

Rada Scenic Art Workshop 03/15

with intense focus, including the challenge of new angles and foreshortenings. Observing the body language of people interacting with each other is especially important in underpinning character-based narrative illustration.

Perhaps the most challenging task of all is that of drawing children. The fact that they are constantly on the move means that it is likely that only the slightest of sketches can be achieved. Speed of eye and thought becomes essential when processing shapes and movements in just a few seconds. This means that it is particularly important to concentrate primarily on overall body shape before attempting too much in the way of facial detail or clothing. Young children are able to sit, move and contort their bodies in ways that are impossible for adults, so once again the process of casting off preconceptions and trusting only the eyes is paramount in order to capture the briefest of moments.

ABOVE: A page from one of Sheila Robinson's sketchbooks from the late 1940s/early 1950s, showing Cromer in Norfolk. Beaches in the summertime are ideal locations for people-watching.

OPPOSITE: Taking children to swimming classes provides a wonderful opportunity to make very quick studies of children and the ways in which they relate to the spaces that they are in, as in these pages from the sketchbook of Jo Spooner.

ABOVE: At this second-hand book fair, I first tried to get a very rough indication of the space 'jotted' in, and then drew the figures as and when they paused to look at books. A drawing such as this, made over about an hour and a half, is, in contrast to a photograph, a synthesis of some of what slowly came and went in front of me over that period of time.

RIGHT: Drawing people from above can very useful in helping to unravel preconceptions about body shape; also, the subjects are less likely to be aware that they are being drawn. I drew these in a shopping mall.

The Basics

Sofa.

OPPOSITE AND TOP: Beatrice Alemagna originally trained in graphic design and typography, and did not receive formal drawing instruction. She has only taken to drawing from direct observation more recently, as in these drawings of her daughter. They demonstrate a fascinating fusion of an already mature illustrative 'voice' with a searching observational eye.

ABOVE: Children move so quickly that it is rare to have the opportunity to make sustained drawings, so speed of eye is paramount. Angela Brooksbank's drawings are full of sensitively observed detail of the shapes and unselfconscious movements that only children can make.

People and environments

Drawing animals

'The shapes being drawn are utterly alien'

One of the best ways to train the eye is to take a drawing trip to a zoo or farm. I have noticed over the years how often illustration students produce some of their best observational drawings when drawing animals and birds directly from life. I have concluded that this must be due to the fact that, most people do not look at live animals every day of their lives, and so the mind surrenders more easily to the fact that the shapes being drawn are utterly alien and more freely allows the eye to take over. An additional factor may be the diminished levels of anxiety about whether or not the subject is aware that it is being drawn!

Becky Brown's drawings of animals and birds from direct observation are not only sharply observed, but exhibit a playful graphic flair for making the most of their dramatic shapes.

The Basics

This sheet of drawings of chickens was made by Paul Hogarth while teaching at Cambridge School of Art. Chickens are something of a gift as a subject for drawing from life, their dramatic shapes being easier to observe as they repeat the same movements over and over again.

ABOVE: Becky Brown's lightning-quick sketches of baby owls and raccoons capture movement and posture as well as an indication of the textures of plumage and fur.

Drawing animals

Drawing and photography

'The camera lens functions in a
very different way to the lens
of the human eye'

'From today, painting is dead.' So, supposedly, said the French painter Paul Delaroche on first setting eyes upon an early daguerreotype photographic print, sometime around 1840. Of course, painting was not about to die; like most advancements in technology and the arts, photography precipitated a different understanding of what art is, who art is for, and, in this instance, what drawing and painting are 'for'. The relationship between drawing and photography is a complex one. But one thing is absolutely clear: it is not possible to learn to draw, in any meaningful sense, through copying photographs. As we have seen, learning to draw by learning to see is a process of developing a visual understanding of form and space, developing skills in processing and translating the complex three-dimensional world into a two-dimensional representation or interpretation. The photograph does most of this for us. A drawing from a photograph involves little more than a process of rendering a surface. And to the trained eye (e.g. someone experienced in drawing from observation) a drawing made from a photographic reference is immediately identifiable as such. We have come to think of the photographic image as synonymous with realistic representation. But the camera lens functions in a very different way to the lens of the human eye. While the human eye will adjust when moving from areas of light to dark shadow, for instance, a camera lens may heighten contrast and leave a blanket of shadow over areas of detail. The wide range of tones that the eye sees in nature is limited in photographic imagery. The shadows that we see in a photograph are not those that we see in the real world.

Of course, photography has been and continues to be an important aid to illustrators in many ways. But for the serious student of drawing, photographic references should be avoided until experience of drawing from life has instilled knowledge and understanding, a healthy mistrust of photographic sources and greater control over how they can be used to supplement and inform.

OPPOSITE: Bernie Fuchs, famed for his advertising and magazine work in the 1950s and 1960s, was known to work regularly from photographic reference material. He was able to do this successfully because he always 'took ownership' of imagery and imposed his own graphic ideas upon his sources.

Where possible, he took his own photographs. The pencil illustration of David Frost and Richard Nixon shown here shows how he exploited graphically the simplified shadows produced by the camera lens. Below is artwork for a magazine illustration, with the rough layout indicated.

CHAPTER 3

From Observation to Imagination

The renowned illustrator–teachers Edward Ardizzone and Lynton Lamb debated the importance or relevance to illustrators of drawing directly from life (see Chapter 1, pp. 38–43). In my own experience, the biggest challenge for most illustration students is that of making natural links between pure observation and imagination. After an intensive period of location drawing, such as a field trip designed specifically for the purpose, or a module or 'unit' in observational drawing, an immediate follow-up project to explore imaginative and narrative responses often causes problems such as excessive dependence on location drawings as reference, or, by contrast, a tendency to immediately dive into over-stylized illustration idioms that apparently owe little or nothing to personal response and the experience of 'being there'.

The underlying reasons for these issues can be found in the nature of our engagement with the subject when drawing on location. If I may try to illustrate this through the use of extremes: at one end of the spectrum, it is possible be a highly skilled analytical draughtsman but to draw in an essentially passive way, delivering a thoroughly competent representation of a chosen view of a three-dimensional subject, but with little or no sense of a personal visual response. At the other end of the spectrum, we may find an approach to observational drawing that is so subjective and emotional that little in the way of actual representational detail is recorded or retained. It is perhaps through the juggling or balancing of these two extremes that a natural way into imaginative illustration through observation is best achieved. To achieve this, in the later stages of the field trip or location drawing project, it is useful to begin to commit scenes and scenarios to visual memory and start drawing them immediately 'after the event'.

Having trained oneself to see more keenly, both through the process of drawing from direct observation and that of 'mentally drawing' everyday scenes and objects when not able to spend time drawing, the next big leap is to inject more of what you *think* and *feel* as well as what you see into your drawing.

The fact that present-day students are exposed to the work of thousands of illustrators from around the world through social media can be both positive and negative. On the one hand, there is now unprecedented instant access to an enormous array of influence from wide-ranging visual cultures and traditions. On the other hand, it is easier than ever to slip into imitative mannerism by (consciously or unconsciously) for example, drawing foliage that owes more to the decorative patterns of a particularly admired picturebook-maker than personal experience of the real world. Developing and drawing from visual memory can help to counter this, not only by building a personal 'library' of forms – the folds in clothes as the wearer's body moves, the shapes of particular plants, trees or buildings – but also by identifying one's own unique visual and social or narrative preoccupations through observing people's gestures and interactions with one another and their environments.

While trying to get to grips with this kind of drawing, it is very easy to become discouraged when drawings emerge that inevitably lack the assurance or 'safety net' of observation. But, as with all drawing, it is essential to persevere. The making of 'bad' drawings is a key component of the learning process.

OPPOSITE: Kristin Roskifte fills sketchbooks with drawings of people, both alone and in groups. For her, drawing from observation, immediate memory or other references has merged into a single language. Her drawings are all based on real people, many of whom find their way into her books.

From Observation to Imagination

Drawing
from memory

'Drawings made from memory are very different...
the drawings will inevitably manifest on paper
in a different way, emerging through the filter
of memory and feelings about the subject'

Successful memory drawing is based on a particularly acute kind of close observation that, for most, has to be learned. Many who aspire to draw well will say that they already take a keen interest in the visual world around them and have no problem in 'seeing'. But learning to look in a way that is specific to the retention of visual information involves, for want of a better term, 'mental drawing'. Notwithstanding Edward Ardizzone's faith in 'drawing a thing over and over again until it looks right' as the method by which illustrators find their way, perhaps the most commonly accepted mantra about the relationship between visual memory and imagination is that 'you cannot draw a thing out of your head if you do not first take the trouble to put it there'. Although such sentiments are firmly rooted in traditions of so-called 'realist' approaches to illustration, they are still relevant in today's world of myriad idiosyncratic visual languages. So the importance of the process of habitual mental drawing cannot be overstated.

When deciding that you are going to draw a particular person or object *after* encountering

it, it is necessary to first learn to look in a very specific way, quickly committing key shapes and their relationships to each other to memory, by imagining that you are drawing them with your eyes and brain rather than with a pencil. Once the inevitably demoralizing early results can be put behind you, perseverance usually pays off. After some time, it becomes increasingly natural and habitual to look in this way: really *seeing* the line of a shoulder through a head, the overall shape of someone bending to pick something up or the unfamiliar outline of a quarter-view face seen from behind, with the tip of the nose just visible beyond the cheekbone. Ardizzone did concede that:

> To acquire a good visual memory and knowledge another practice is essential: the practice of really looking at things and trying to commit them to memory. In this context the keeping of an illustrated diary helps enormously. If every young student would jot down something of what happens to him or interests him each day and illustrate it with a small drawing done from memory, he would

OPPOSITE: Edward Ardizzone was a great champion of the anecdotal visual journal, and kept one himself.

His *Diary of a Holiday Afloat* was published in the eleventh issue of the popular *Saturday Book* (Hutchinson, 1951).

find the combination of words and drawing a most useful exercise.

Over time, as this process of building ways of seeing and resultant visual knowledge evolves, the registering of tone, colour and atmosphere – the more subjective responses – become increasingly important. Drawings made from memory are very different in nature from those made from observation. Even if the intention had been to convey a scene as accurately as possible, the drawings will inevitably manifest on paper in a different way, emerging through the filter of memory and feelings about the subject. The line itself will be imbued with a different character, often revealing new possibilities and directions. As this approach to drawing matures, it can in turn feed back into direct observational drawing.

'Drawing…is very much in connection with you and your feeling and your mood, and the result is affected by it'

Yann Kebbi
An organic approach

The symbiosis between observation and imagination for many illustrators is particularly well evidenced through the work of artist, illustrator and graphic novelist Yann Kebbi. At a time when editorial illustration in particular can look somewhat 'flat', the organic aesthetic of his work stands out as determinedly and defiantly *drawn*. The connections between his sketchbooks and his published works are clearly evident, but perhaps more complex than at first sight.

Kebbi initially studied Applied Art, which he says gave him a good foundation, followed by a two-year degree in Illustration, both at École Estienne with a six-month exchange stay at Parsons School in New York City. He then studied at the École Nationale Supérieure des Arts Décoratifs, where he says the fields were more integrated. '*I kept on pushing and finding my thing and doing other processes like etching, monoprint, silkscreen printing, digital…*'.

Kebbi draws a great deal in his sketchbooks on location. In an interview with the Cartoon Museum of Basel, he explains:

When you draw from life, there is a moment, sometimes you're in the subway or you're outside, it starts raining, you are forced to draw – it's not like being in the studio with a sheet of paper…. Everything is interesting to draw, it's just a matter of how you are going to represent or approach it…. But they nourish each other. If I feel my studio work is getting a bit 'lazy', I go back outside. But for narrative work I don't do a 'research phase' where I draw outside and take the drawings back to the studio to work from.

Elaborating on his drawing-based, organic approach to illustration, Kebbi says:

My main concern is with the process of drawing itself. I think this organic feeling comes from the fact that my images are constructed with the intention of keeping it partly 'sketchy' or not hiding the process of construction, but also from the fact that in the 'illustration world' of images applied to a purpose like editorial or communication, something very easy to read is expected. I guess observation has been the main influence on that lively approach, but also the

idea of not being too conformist, and is varying the techniques, scale, applications of contexts where my works could evolve.

Am I both a 'fine artist' and an 'illustrator'? That's a distinction I have trouble making, but I guess the straight answer is 'yes'. I think the two, if they were to be compared, are intertwined. For me it is more a matter of 'where the drawing/image is going to be used', which of course influences the result. I truly believe doing just one thing, evolving in just one of these 'frames' is both frustrating and limiting – creatively and financially.

Maybe this assertion comes from the fact that I am not a good illustrator, in the sense that communicating a clear idea isn't really a big concern. I think conveying an emotion, a feeling, something funny, abstract, is more important and should be more looked for in editorial works. In that regard, I think my work might, maybe, cross more easily the bridge of 'illustration' to 'fine art', as it is more focused on the form and what that form conveys than using codes to create a meaning. You also go

Above: An editorial illustration from *M le Magazine du Monde,* on the subject of picnicking.
Following page: From *Howdy,* an exhibition and book based on Kebbi's three-month
road trip across America (Galerie Champaka, Paris, 2015).

Yann Kebbi

where people accept your work, I think... I really don't like that separation between 'illustration' and 'fine arts', I believe this is an old debate that has very little to do with the reality of the process.

Working to commission is very exciting, it is a challenge, because the timing is short, because someone directly contacts you and recognizes a sense in your work enough to ask you to create. It can also be very frustrating when either the brief isn't easy to adapt, or is very directed. The art director feels your work would match a subject, so they project something onto the result. That allows efficiency, but also creates a big problem for me: it doesn't allow you to evolve. And that's fine, it just means, in my opinion, that it is not in regular commissioned work that your drawing can evolve. And evolving is

imperative in my opinion. What's the point of doing the same thing over and over again? You grow weary.

Drawing, or creating in a more general way, is a very instinctive process, a need. So it means it is very much in connection with you and your feeling and your mood, and the result is affected by it. So there is something strange to me in trying to control the result at all cost. I am not speaking about narrative processes like comic books for example. That is an entirely different matter for me, in the fact that the drawing is there to support a story.

To be honest, it is not often that I feel truly satisfied with a commissioned work compared to a drawing I would do for something I truly believe in. But again, I think the two are intertwined, because it is 'personal work'

that brings the commission in the first place, and sometimes the work that is commissioned allows you to take time for more personal work. It's a back and forth.

I believe a good drawing is lively. I think movement is the key, in the process and in the result. Things that are too tight, too nice, I don't know...it is dangerous to produce something too sophisticated, you can end up trapped. Actually, my drawings are often quite constructed and thought out in advance, so if I was a bit cynical I'd say that apparent 'raw' quality is in fact a trick. But balancing the aim of a communicative drawing, applied to a purpose, with maintaining a sense of exploration isn't easy, because in a way the two things are kind of opposite.

What does 'drawing' mean to me? It's a necessity.

From Observation to Imagination

Top: Sketchbook pages.
Above: A spread from Kebbi's graphic novel *Lontano: Fondation Kebbi* (Actes Sud, 2019).

Yann Kebbi

Simon Bartram
Monday Man

One of the most outstanding draughtsmen working in illustration today, Simon Bartram is a highly successful picturebookmaker, best known for his book series featuring 'Bob' the genial astronaut and his football-related children's books, such as *Up for the Cup!* (Templar, 2014). Figure drawing has always been central to his practice as an illustrator, but in recent years he has also taken time to work solely for himself. His visual ideas predominantly take the form of intense busts or full-figure studies of men from his native northeast England.

'I always wanted to "do art"', he says, 'but I didn't really know how to go about it as a career. I just wanted to draw.' He had been a keen consumer of comics in childhood and, as an avid football fan, had been especially devoted to Roy of the Rovers. But the idea of it being possible to be an illustrator only really occurred to him when seeing the signatures of artists next to their work: 'One of the first to register with me was Schiaffino, who drew Hotshot Hamish. He studied Visual Communication at Birmingham School of Art, where he says he went to as many extra evening classes in life drawing as he could; now, he works almost entirely from memory.

Here, he explains what the 'discipline' of drawing, in both its literal and broader sense, means to him in relation to personal work and applied illustration.

My approach to the discipline of drawing can be varied. Indeed, the amount of 'discipline' required depends on the purpose of the drawing. If I am working on a study for a subsequent painting, I tend to carefully render a detailed, linear, almost technical sketch that will function as a skeleton for the picture. Such drawings are meticulously plotted. I know the destination and I will refine it until I achieve my goal.

However, lots of other drawings, particularly those in sketchbooks, require much less 'discipline'. In fact, for me, they require a certain 'switching off' of conscious discipline. The shackles fall away and drawing takes place for drawing's sake without it being a cog in a bigger project. Muscle memory takes over and I tend not to tighten up or worry. The destination of the drawing is unclear, which is very liberating. Often, nothing good emerges, which is fine as all that has been invested is a little time. However, sometimes, a little gem might appear, and it may surprise you and lead you along new paths in

the future. In this regard sketchbooks are vital. From the first page to the last, small, incremental changes to style or technique or colour can add up to a bigger, almost unconscious change to the direction of your work.

The drawing shown here was one of six I did one Monday morning. Four of them ended up in the bin. Two of them I was pleased with. A lot of my pictures at the moment feature a certain kind of male face. I enjoy playing with proportions. This one was drawn from my imagination using charcoal and carbon pencils. It is roughly A3 in size. Other times I will work from a piece of reference material, although rarely will I slavishly reproduce a photo. Reality always needs a tweak in my opinion, even if it's just a little tweak.

For most of my adult life I have worked as an illustrator, particularly in the field of children's books. More recently, however, I have been working on a series of personal painting projects. For many years I have had a backlog of pictures building up in my head and I feel now is the right time to get them down in paint.

From Observation to Imagination

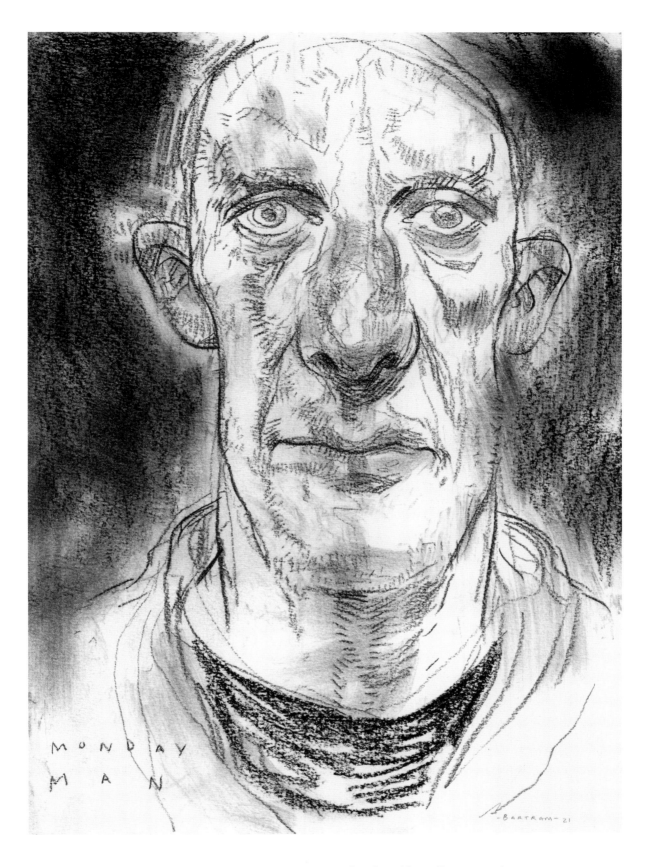

Above: In recent years, Simon Bartram has found himself increasingly
engaged with self-directed drawings and paintings of a particular type
of male head, which he explores with intense focus and detail.

Simon Bartram

115

Bill Bragg
Making the links

Bill Bragg's award-winning work across book and editorial illustration, graphic novels, painting and most recently children's picturebooks is widely admired. His imaginative, atmospheric artwork is rooted in sound draughtsmanship and design, and his carefully considered views on the relationship between observation and imagination in visual thinking are highly illuminating. Bragg's father was a graphic designer and his mother an art teacher with a love of drawing and painting. He feels that his own work quite naturally straddles those two fields. Drawing was encouraged, but never forcibly so:

I was into all sorts of things. I loved making things, always using my hands. My parents had a nice way of encouraging subtly: they would leave things lying around for me to look at that they thought might interest me – design magazines, articles and so on. And I grew up aware of the lifestyle of freelance work, my father's studio full of

fascinating equipment and materials lying around – French curves and so on that would frequently 'find their way' into my bedroom.

At school he always felt that others were technically 'better at drawing' than he was: *'But I enjoyed it beyond the technical proficiency side – it was the adventure of drawing really.'* He enrolled on the Art Foundation course at Newcastle-under-Lyme Art School and, like many others, found this stage of art school education particularly joyful:

It was a fantastic course. Drawing ran through everything – life drawing, location drawing and experimenting with all sorts of media and processes. And the fun and camaraderie of everyone doing what they love. I didn't really come out of the sketchbook at that stage. I did also do a lot of photography, and photography has continued to be a significant influence on my work – Josef Koudelka, for example, his way of his way of composing images and graphic use of light and shadow.

After Foundation, Bragg studied Illustration as a main option within Communication Design at Central Saint Martins in London. He continued to work predominantly in sketchbooks. Sharing accommodation with jazz musicians, he found himself doing a lot of drawing at jazz gigs, where it was too dark to see the paper of his sketchbook and he was forced to draw 'blind', one of the most intense forms of observational drawing. Later, while studying for his MA at the Royal College of Art, one drawing project had particular significance for Bragg with regard to the key issue for many illustrators: linking observation and imagination as naturally and organically as possible. In this three-stage project, the students were first given a list of interesting, iconic places and buildings in London along with detailed written descriptions of each, their histories and functions, and invited to make drawings from the descriptions. Stage two involved visiting the actual locations and

Above: Linking observation and imagination has played a key role in the
evolution of Bill Bragg's illustration work, as seen in these images of Wilton's
Music Hall, London, made while Bragg was a student at the Royal College of Art.

Bill Bragg

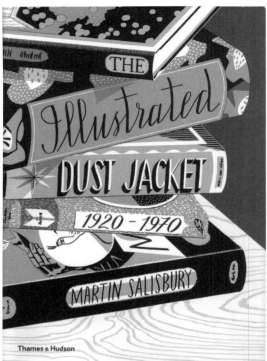

drawing directly from observation. The final stage of the project required the students to make drawings of the venues back in the studio, from memory. As Bragg explains, the project cleverly facilitated the building of links between imagination, observation and memory: 'There was something quite scientific about it in a way, exploring emotions, atmosphere, sight…understanding that we are always using one or other of these.'

Projects such as these, underpinned by long periods as a student spent enjoying 'the luxury of being able to draw from life and experiment and play in the sketchbook' have played a key role in forming Bragg's working methods when drawing for illustration as a professional illustrator today:

Now when I begin work on a project, I always draw from imagination first,

'feeling' my way into it. There's a kind of 'muscle memory' at work – hand and brain. Of course, there will then often be the need for more information, and so I have to go back to observation or reference. Occasionally, if the time and place of the subject is unfamiliar, there is a need for research at the start but usually there is a way in.

When illustrating Kafka's Metamorphosis and Other Stories for the Folio Society, I found myself basing the setting and the atmosphere of one particular illustration on a place I remember from childhood. I was then able to 'layer on' the specific period detail. Creating a convincing illusion is the key thing. Sometimes there needs to be a degree of visual 'truth' underpinning the emotional truth. I guess it's a bit like staging a play, the need for a certain amount of authentic

detail. Light is very important. A shadow or reflection invites the viewer to imagine its source and gives a sense of there being a larger world beyond the frame. The balance of light and shadow and how it can be used to strengthen a composition is something I often think about. For this reason, my initial sketches are always in black and white. I think the influence of photography comes through here again.

As an illustrator you could be required to draw anything, and this can often feel quite daunting. Even after twenty yearsl rarely feel confident before I start a project and often think 'I don't know whether I can do this'. But once I start, the feelings of trepidation fall away as I become absorbed and transported by what I'm drawing. When I get 'in the zone' the hours disappear.

Opposite: The preparatory rough (left) for Bragg's front cover (right)
for *The Illustrated Dust Jacket: 1920–1970* (Thames & Hudson, 2017).
Above: The strong sense of place in this sketch of Erith Yacht Club
grows from a particular, personal connection with the location.

Bill Bragg

Above and opposite: Bragg's preliminary sketch and final digital artwork
for Arthur Conan-Doyle's 'The Captain of the Pole-Star', in *Ghostly Tales:
Spine-Chilling Stories of the Victorian Age* (Chronicle Books, 2017).

From Observation to Imagination

Bill Bragg

Sketchbooks, visual journals and doodles

'In this private world we can take risks, make "mistakes", make "bad" drawings and mess, explore the properties of different tools and materials without fear of judgment'

For many illustrators, the sketchbook is the place where the personal visual vocabulary begins to assert itself, a private place where drawing from direct observation can mix freely with flights of visual fancy, doodles, notes, uninhibited mark-making, shopping lists and bus tickets. Doodles are especially important. As with handwriting, each individual will tend to display a particular graphic identity when making marks on paper while their primary concentration is perhaps on something other than the marks themselves. Some will doodle controlled geometric shapes, others softly flowing rhythmic patterns. Some doodles may form into pictorial representations simply by building on unexpected connections. Many will remain abstract. But in any event, this process of 'unconscious' and unselfconscious mark-making can play an important role in underpinning the illustrator's emerging visual language.

Each of us will use the sketchbook in our own particular way. For most of us, whether as amateurs, students or professionals, drawing is as fraught with psychological issues as it is with those of a technical or practical nature – fear of failure and being judged, self-consciousness – the outcomes being tied up with a sense of self-worth. But in this private world we can take risks, make 'mistakes', make 'bad' drawings and mess, explore the properties of different tools and materials without fear of judgment. There is always a danger of wanting to 'make a beautiful book' and this usually leads to a completely counterproductive paralysis. Not everyone likes to work in sketchbooks, and many professional illustrators no longer have time to use them. But for many, especially students and other learners, they are the key to progress, as a place where the things that interest us visually, emotionally and conceptually can be recorded, played around with, mixed up, developed and occasionally reflected upon. Crucially, the sketchbook is often the place where natural links are made between observation and imagination or memory, and therefore much of what goes on in there will find its way, directly or indirectly, into later applied work.

OPPOSITE: These linear doodles were made by illustrator and educator Nigel Robinson during an art-school board meeting. They meander between the abstract and geometric, pattern-making and representation.

From Observation to Imagination

ABOVE AND OPPOSITE: Pages from Hayley Wells's sketchbook, showing the close relationship between drawing from observation and developing character studies for narrative illustration, alongside detailed colour planning.

From Observation to Imagination

OPPOSITE: The edges of a stretched sheet of watercolour paper, outside the image area, are often used to test the colours and tonality of washes. Here, James Dawson's test marks gradually formed themselves into an extended pictorial doodle.

TOP: Part of a page of studies for a narrative illustration project by Gill Smith.

ABOVE: A spread from Marina Ruiz's sketchbook. Sensitively rendered experiments with pencil and watercolour are scattered with notes and *aides mémoire*.

Sketchbooks, visual journals and doodles   127

John Vernon Lord
The journals

In his dual roles as former Professor of Illustration at the University of Brighton and a leading illustrator whose award-winning projects have included the 'unillustratable' James Joyce novels *Ulysses* and *Finnegans Wake* and his own best-selling picturebook, *The Giant Jam Sandwich*, John Vernon Lord is a much-loved influence on the illustration world. Alongside his illustration practice and his work in higher education, he has kept personal journals, diaries and notebooks in one form or another since his days as a student at Salford Art College in the late 1950s. He confesses to being obsessive about these and unable to break the habit. He says that on the rare occasions that he revisits them, he is invariably disappointed by them, echoing André Gide's observations of his journals:

What good is this journal? I cling to these pages as to something fixed among so many fugitive things. I oblige myself to write anything whatever in them just so I do it regularly every day.

But for the observer, the privilege of a glimpse into this private world reveals much about the way Vernon Lord's visual vocabulary has evolved, and about the importance of the activity rather reductively termed 'doodling'. He perfectly sums up the desire harboured by so many, to transfer more of the characteristically unselfconscious mark-making of the sketchbook or notebook into the arena of the 'finished' illustration for reproduction:

Over the years I have doodled at many meetings at art college, polytechnic and university. It is a compulsion that I can hardly avoid. Doodling is a way of aiding concentration and it soothes any tension that sometimes arises during a discussion. The spontaneous action of doodling not only helps me listen and take in what is being said but it also assists my own involvement in discussion. It is therefore important that I do not take the doodle too seriously as to its quality. It must be aimless and I must not improve it or worry about how well or badly it is developing during the drawing of it. Doodles have a private life of their own, and they more or less draw themselves. Perhaps some of our creative expression comes from our unconscious minds.

The themes of an agenda item, or a remark, might prompt me to come up with symbols related to the discussion at hand during a meeting, but some of the doodles are populated with meanings and significances that I have now largely forgotten about. Some of the images, however, are capable of bringing a meeting vividly back to life! The doodles do not necessarily relate to the essence of a meeting, but now and again a frustration may be evident.

Consistent images are constantly brought to the surface when doodling. Prevailing symbols seem to appear regularly, and I cannot account for this. There are men with elaborate hats, wearing ruffs, and many sporting a wide range of moustaches. Fish feature a lot too, as do birds. Many doodles are populated with pencils and pens; sometimes these instruments are seen in the act of drawing or writing independently, without the help of a guiding hand. Wine glasses and cups keep appearing, as well as buildings and doorways. Letters and numbers crop up regularly. Arrows, darts, screws, nails and keys are frequently employed as penetrating instruments. Question marks and exclamation marks are regular signs that turn up in doodles. Plants, trees, books and shoes seem to be favoured subjects too. Light bulbs shine forth and sometimes little explosions take place. I do not care to interpret these symbols for myself or attempt to unveil their meanings. That is for others.

The doodles are essentially aimless drawings. They allow for a great deal of intuition, which my illustrations so often lack in terms of graphic approach. They release in me a kind of automatic drawing that the illustrator in me envies.

From Observation to Imagination

Above and following spread: Pages from John Vernon Lord's numerous notebooks and diaries. Vernon Lord has kept highly individual, intensely detailed illustrated journals for most of his adult life, each carefully numbered and dated. They form a unique record of a lifetime of drawing, illustrating and teaching. They also illustrate the importance of thinking through drawing. These pages come from 1976, 2002, 2004 and 2008, and were published in *John's Journal Jottings* (Inky Parrot Press, 2009).

John Vernon Lord

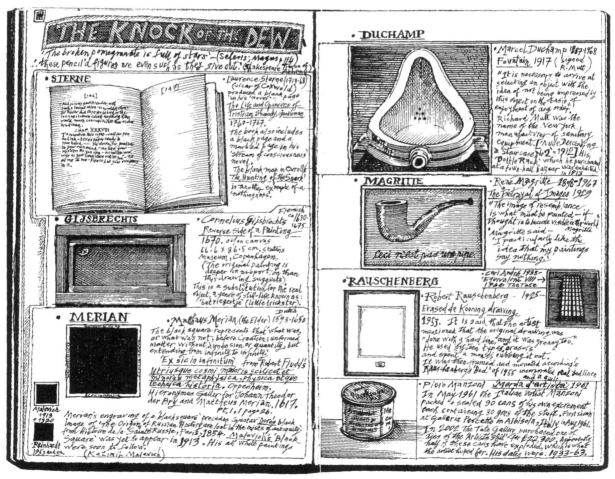

A fisherman catches a fish and during the discharging process of the hook the longish fish swallows the fisherman's hand. The fisherman spends several embarrassed days with a fish at the end of his right hand — shaking "hands" with visitors, fishy smell, cats after him in the street etc. Finally the unfortunate man plunges in the pond and is never seen again

sleeps at night with hand in jam jar to keep the poor fish alive.

fissure. fisher of men

STARTLING
STARTLING
STARING
STRING
STING
SING
SIN
IN
I

> 'I am continuously learning from the preliminary drawings found in the sketchbooks of great artists such as Anthony van Dyck, Käthe Kollwitz and J. M. W. Turner'

Sally Dunne
Sketchbooks and me

After winning the Victoria and Albert Museum Student Illustrator of the Year Award in 2020 with her illustrations from the Kakuma refugee camp in Kenya, Sally Dunne has gone on to work on a number of high-profile commissions with the Folio Society. The first, published in 2021, was to illustrate Agatha Christie's *Crooked House*, one of the author's own favourite novels. Her cover design was executed in watercolour and the interior illustrations in pastel and pencil. She followed this up immediately by tackling Georgette Heyer's 1958 Regency romance, *Venetia*, also in pastels, which she describes as challenging, but from which she feels she has learned a great deal.

Dunne is an illustrator for whom drawing and observation are particularly crucial. She is a prolific sketchbook user, which forms a foundation to her approach to illustration in general.

My sketchbooks are often filled with a combination of visual notes, drawings from life, imagined characters, compositional ideas and developing storyboards. I keep a sketchbook with me wherever I go, in case an idea springs to mind, or a particular landscape, character or moment captures my attention. These studies may later inspire a more finished piece of work.

I would consider some of my sketchbooks to be visual diaries that reveal subconscious motifs. For this reason, it can feel quite daunting exhibiting or sharing them with others! However, I do feel that revealing the working process can be an invaluable resource for others. When an artist exhibits or shares their sketchbooks, they are revealing their scruffy workings-out, preliminary sketches, the gradual evolution of an imagined character or the germ of an idea that is yet to be fully realized. I am continuously learning from the preliminary drawings found in the sketchbooks of great artists such as Anthony van Dyck, Käthe Kollwitz and J. M. W. Turner.

I draw from life as much as possible, as I find that details from sketchbook studies of landscapes, portraits and interiors can inspire or contribute authentically to an imagined world. For example, I am particularly fascinated by the various ways that light and shadow informs and enhances the atmosphere and emotion in an image. With my sketchbook to hand, I can quickly note down, for instance, how sunlight casts particular shadows on grass or how it highlights a person's face and the folds in their clothing. I can later utilize these details in my imagined work to help make the fictional world I am drawing look more convincing or believable.

Working in sketchbooks is an invaluable part of my practice for three main reasons. The first and perhaps most immediate reason is the functionality of a sketchbook. Its portability enables me to take visual notes anywhere. Secondly, the privacy of a sketchbook can encourage naturally cautious illustrators like myself to try out ideas within the secure parameters of the pages. I feel I create some of my best and most uninhibited work in my sketchbooks. On occasion, I have started a small drawing in the corner of my sketchbook that spontaneously developed into a finished piece of artwork, an unexpected but ultimately very satisfying result. Finally, a sketchbook is an insightful visual record of the artist's working process that can be very instructive and valuable for other artists. We are able to observe the sketchbook owner's technique and follow their thought processes. Through studying their preliminary drawings, we can understand and observe how their initial studies progressed into final works of art.

Sketchbooks can also encourage the illustrator to creatively organize and arrange their ideas. Working in a sketchbook is an exciting opportunity to design, collage and arrange information. Many pages of my sketchbooks are crammed full with seemingly random combinations of individual, observed or imagined studies. Sometimes I will find ways to visually link these separate ideas retrospectively in order to discover a connecting theme or idea.

A sketchbook is a private place to experiment. This can feel very liberating, as we do not have to consider an audience's opinion of our work. For this reason, there is a risk that our best work remains hidden away within their safe boundaries. We may also encounter a common dilemma: 'how do I recreate the same energy and spontaneity in the final artwork?

From Observation to Imagination

Above and following spread: Sally Dunne's pocket-sized sketchbooks always accompany her, and are used for multiple forms of information-gathering and idea-developing. Direct observational studies are mixed with quick visual idea notes and occasional highly finished artworks.

Sally Dunne

but they were a lot too close for comfort and Tino felt out of his depth.

Alexis Deacon
Drawing, thinking and the psychology of 'finished'

Alexis Deacon is widely admired for his astonishing, almost anachronistic drawing skills, generally executed with a humble pencil. Of the leading illustrators of today, it could perhaps be argued that Deacon is one for whom the line between drawing for illustration and drawing as illustration becomes most blurred. He grew up in an artistic family and says that he was 'always obsessed with drawing'. His sculptor father's studio was outside the home, but he was allowed to be there and get on with drawing and 'not be a burden'.

When, after graduating from art school, his first encounters with publishers invariably led to feedback on his 'finished' illustrations being along the lines of 'can you make it more like your sketchbooks', he developed strategies for limiting the steps between first marks and 'finals'. It is a scenario that may be only too familiar to many who struggle to retain in their illustration work the vitality of the very first exploratory marks. Those much-admired sketchbooks are used less now, and in different ways:

I don't really use sketchbooks so much now. They were talismanic things.... But I didn't want to get into that 'show us your sketchbook, who's got the best sketchbook' competitive thing. After a period when I couldn't work because of an illness, I decided I wanted my illustration work to be the sketchbooks. Now they are more of a support tool. I do have one with me most days, just for getting something down when needed — filling in gaps in knowledge.

You have these problems in your head, stuff that you've tried to draw and struggled with, you see something and think 'that would make a fantastic drawing' and if you don't have any materials with you, you just try to memorize what you can in the moment. I think it helps if you've had a specific problem or question and then you see the answer to it out in the world.

Looking back to those early encounters with publishers, I think I internalized it. I did see the sense in it. Once I'd embraced why they were responding better to the original sketch, I sort of made it a life's mission to try and invent processes that allow me to remain as close to that original moment as possible. I think it's maybe something to do with what Ardizzone was getting at — when you're drawing the rough, if you're an illustrator of a certain type, the story's happening, you know — it's happening in front of your eyes. And you're making a lot of intuitive decisions about how big something is, what else is present in the scene, what position they're in, and everything is narrative because you are just trying to tell the story, that's your only concern. And then the more times you try to draw it over again, the more distant you get from that moment of creation in response to the narrative, the more redundant considerations and those questions of self-worth and craftsmanship and so on start to creep in. It took me a long time to realize that things that didn't take ages to do had value. I still think I hide behind technique sometimes — I still want to impress people at heart. Working in animation and comics more recently has been very effective in breaking some of those things down, because the demands of the schedule are such that you either 'get it' in the time that you have, or you don't. There's no time for fretting, you're just on to the next thing.

Soonchild was published by Walker Books in 2012. The author, Russell Hoban,

From Observation to Imagination

Above: A page from one of Alexis Deacon's sketchbooks, showing working notes, dialogues and the kinds of drawings that proved impossible to better or replicate in his final illustrations, leading him to create strategies to cut out the 'leap' from sketchbook to final piece. Following spread and pp. 140–41: Examples of Alexis Deacon's original drawings for *Soonchild* (text by Russell Hoban, Walker Books, 2012), used as the final artworks for the book, shown with the printed spreads.

Alexis Deacon

From Observation to Imagination

JOHN AND RAVEN GET SUCKED IN

John and Raven didn't have to find the Point of Suction, it came looking for them and it sucked them in. Oh, the wetness of it and the smell! Like some bigger-than-the-world problem with drains, whether blocked or un-blocked it would be hard to say. "Wait a minute!" shouted John amid the horrendous ulping and gulping.

"For what?" said Raven. "A belch?"

"We're already being swallowed by Yiwok! I felt us go over a great slobbery lower lip!"

"Duck!" said Raven as a herd of cows scrabbled over them, followed by a tractor, a chicken house, forty or fifty rolls of barbed wire, a symphony orchestra playing a symphony and two lovers in the act of love.

"We're on the enormous tongue," said John. "Here comes throat and we're going throoooouuugh!"

Alexis Deacon

died before the book was published, but not before he had received a printed copy. His particular brand of magic realism provided plenty of scope for Deacon to use the full range of his visual vocabulary. Over sixty illustrations, ranging from full double-page spreads to small 'drop-ins', are arranged throughout the text (originally written as a freestanding work) with an element of visual pace that contributes to the sense of increasing drama.

I think it was Walker who suggested illustrations. Hoban was very supportive. He'd worked with many other illustrators and he had been an illustrator himself once, a very good one. He was very open to collaboration. There were occasionally things that

he suggested or vetoed but he was pretty 'hands-off' most of the time.

Usually when I'm given a text I try to think about what illustration might add to it. And one of the things I noticed when reading Soonchild was that the progression of the text wasn't obviously narrative. It was quite episodic. So I wanted to give the audience a feeling that they were moving towards something, and that things were escalating. Actually, I now realize that there is escalation in the text. But the gathering pace in the illustration was intentional.

The background tints of colour were suggested by Ben Norland (the book's designer). We wanted to mark phases in the text – it's about a shaman quest, and he goes deeper

and deeper into this world to fix a problem that he's made by being an awful shaman. So we wanted to somehow mark when a threshold had been crossed.

There were certain points that I felt were more important than others. Again, I feel this is something that illustrations can really help with. It's like 'searing' certain moments in an audience's mind so that they can mark them as significant because they're going to be 'called back'. So certain moments stand out and of course some you just feel 'I really must draw that'. The section where he dies I felt was the axis of the book, so I treated it almost like a picturebook sequence.

For the drawings for Soonchild, Deacon used a combination of charcoal, pencil and

　　　　　From Observation to Imagination

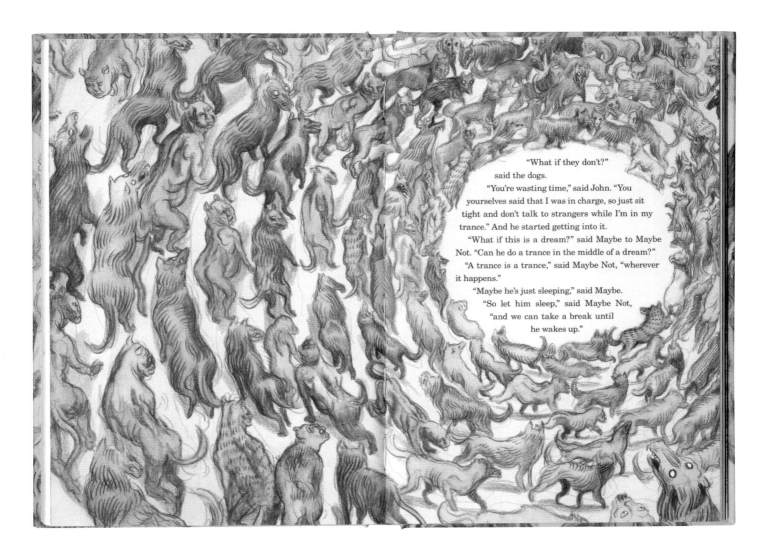

Inside the illustration:

"What if they don't?" said the dogs.

"You're wasting time," said John. "You yourselves said that I was in charge, so just sit tight and don't talk to strangers while I'm in my trance." And he started getting into it.

"What if this is a dream?" said Maybe to Maybe Not. "Can he do a trance in the middle of a dream?"

"A trance is a trance," said Maybe Not, "wherever it happens."

"Maybe he's just sleeping," said Maybe.

"So let him sleep," said Maybe Not, "and we can take a break until he wakes up."

---

aquarelle pencil. Charcoal predominated, with drawings made at a larger scale and heavily reduced. That, he says, dictated aspects of how the illustrations would look: 'Charcoal's a good medium for large scale, it works very comfortably. I mix scales so it's not immediately too obvious at what scale it was drawn'. He works standing up at an angled architect's drawing table – originally for physical reasons, but as time has gone by, just through preference. Pencil and charcoal continue to be his first love:

With the comic that I've been working on recently I started working with ink and brush, but then I switched to pencil on a sort of drafting film to get a very dark line, so that it wouldn't be a problem for reproduction.

I much prefer the sensation of drawing with a pencil or charcoal as compared to ink because I like the grading, the pressure. Pressure is such an important part of the way I draw and I haven't been able to replicate that with a brush (except with a brush-pen that's just about to run out, and at that point you have the same flexibility of making a mark that can be either very, very light or very bold). The humble pencil – you go through phases of becoming particularly fond of one or other. I suppose seventy to eighty per cent of my thinking is in line.

I don't know – those lines...the moment of creation of a story...the feeling that you get when you're making a mark, the emotional connection that you feel as you are drawing,

that's always felt like the essential part of it to me. Then the rest of it is just 'add-ons' – for example if there has to be colour or it has to be a certain shape or size according to the publishers' demands, you just do the minimum necessary to get through. The act of drawing has always been the essential thing for me. It's the bit that I enjoy the most and that's where the value is.

CHAPTER 4

Drawing and Applied Illustration

The ways in which drawing relates to illustration are many, both in a general sense and also in the way approaches and attitudes to drawing differ from illustrator to illustrator, as we have seen throughout the previous sections of this book. For some professional practitioners, drawing feeds seamlessly into their applied illustration work and illustration feeds back equally seamlessly into drawing. For others, the connection is more nuanced. Now that illustrators have such a range of possible media and platforms at their disposal – digital and traditional – this can be particularly apparent. Drawing in the literal sense may not be explicitly visible in the end product, but its presence may be manifest in the underlying draughtsmanship that anchors its design and construction. The act of drawing in the more literal sense may be used for primarily functional purposes, testing ideas and approaches that cannot be fully evaluated until they are roughed out in visual form. The analogy with poetry is perhaps once again relevant here. The expression 'How can I know what I think until I see what I say?' has been attributed to various writers including E. M. Forster and Graham Wallas, although both credited it originally to André Gide, himself quoting an apocryphal old lady who was pooh-poohing the idea of logic. It resonates naturally with the concept of 'thinking through drawing' – drawn lines or written words forming on paper, needing to be seen, heard out loud and 'felt' as they emerge, often surprising their author and impacting on the subsequent direction of the drawing or poem.

In its final form, modern illustration can often be shape-based in execution rather than relying on the ubiquitous line of previous generations. This seems to be the case particularly in editorial work, where strong and simple graphic shapes currently predominate, especially on screen. Many of the artists in this field work digitally, while others fuse digital technology with traditional approaches such as printmaking, creating effects that are informed by and refer back to processes such as screenprinting, lithography and linocut. Jon McNaught's work can be seen as an example of such fusion.

In narrative and sequential illustration, such as authorial picturebooks and graphic novels, whatever medium or media the artist uses for the final work, drawing still plays a key role in developing page designs, balancing visual pace and structure and especially in developing convincing characterization. One of the most common remarks one hears from working illustrators is along the lines of 'I wish I had more time to draw from observation'. But for most, it is the intense period of drawing during their formal art education that forms the foundation of everything that they do today. Many speak of 'muscle memory' or use the analogy of driving a car to describe the unconscious, tacit knowledge that long hours of drawing from observation has instilled deep within them. The diverse and wide-ranging application of drawing to applied illustration is examined in this final chapter primarily through the observations of individual specialist practitioners.

OPPOSITE: A page from Jon McNaught's graphic novel *Dockwood* (Nobrow, 2012).

Editorial and magazine illustration

'A field of illustration that demands not just a solid grounding in drawing, but an ability to digest and process written arguments or speculations in often arcane subject areas'

The term 'editorial illustration' is used to describe illustration that is commissioned to accompany writing in newspapers and magazines. Its function is partly to give some visual impact to a page that would otherwise be very text-heavy, but also to supply a visual interpretation of the content of an article that may be dealing with, for example, abstract concepts or debates and opinions around politics, finance, science, sport or culture and society. It is a field of illustration that demands not just a solid grounding in drawing, but an ability to digest and process written arguments or speculations in often arcane subject areas and represent them through imagery that gives a clear visual 'way in' to the topic.

This area is one that very often requires the artist to employ visual metaphor in order to distil the text elegantly into a single image that embodies the concepts explored. Often, this can involve the use of figures of speech, which are themselves often very visual ('digging a hole for himself', 'it's raining cats and dogs', 'I felt like a fish out of water'). Food and lifestyle illustration has tended to be superseded by photography in publications in the recent past, but historically these have also been important mainstays for illustrators. For much of the last century, magazine and journal covers were also adorned with bespoke commissioned illustrations, providing a major platform for artists in times of high circulation. Special supplements in newspapers or magazines such as Christmas Specials, 'The Book Supplement' or 'Travel Special' continue to be sources of work for editorial illustrators, with art editors keen to make these sections stand out visually as much as possible.

OPPOSITE: The illustrator and printmaker Robert Tavener designed numerous excellent covers for magazines through the mid-twentieth century.

FOLLOWING SPREAD: For much of the last century, many illustrators were kept in regular work by popular magazines, especially for short romantic fiction. This spread is by Trevor Willoughby for a 1957 edition of *Homes and Gardens*.

waiting

BY VERONICA HENRIQUES

A T FOUR o'clock there would at least be some music. Her pacing could alternate to the rhythm of the music. It was just hungry pacing now, wanting, wanting, wanting, moving, to keep the wanting in control.

It wouldn't matter if it were dance music or not. In fact, it would be better if they played a symphony, for then she could accompany the sound with all her body, and heart and thoughts. Or if only they would play that concerto which she and Peter had heard together when they drove through the sinews of the world on that moonlit night, when the mountains were mourning in everlasting time.

Except it wasn't in this world that they had been. It was in some other world where only the immortal existed; immortal music, immortal thinking, immortal beauty like the moon and the mountains, and a wind was just there, coming from no particular direction, to drug the air, then rush with it into their lungs, filling them, oh, filling them until they could burst with awe at the sight of such a wonderful and lovely world.

At four o'clock there would be music. At five, he would come.

"I always get home at five," he had said, "and so, when you call on

Illustrated by

"I've come to see Peter," said Lillian. "He does live here?" "Yes, he does," Jane replied, "but he's not in at the moment."

Trevor Willoughby

'When a client sends an editorial commission, I will grab a pencil, open my sketchbook and read the text. My head is filled with random imagery and concepts as I read the article, and I make quick thumbnail sketches as I read'

David Humphries Newton's Cradle or 'the biggest hum'

David Humphries studied Illustration at Cambridge and Central Saint Martin's schools of art. Drawing from observation played a major role in his early art education. A large part of his work as an illustrator now is within editorial illustration for newspapers and magazines. Here, he explains in detail the subtle connections between a background in drawing and the ability to explore and creatively exploit the complex visual grammar of this field of illustration. The drawing shown opposite is from an intensely personal series that he made as a student and while his father was in hospital.

My dad suffered a serious brain injury while I was at college. Initially he was in a coma, and he remained in hospital for a considerable time. I was very close to my dad, and I have never had the ability to describe the pain and trauma in words. It wasn't a conscious decision to draw him. At the time, I drew constantly and I took my sketchbook everywhere. It didn't occur to me not to draw him.

I love that everyone can draw, and drawings can be enjoyed by everyone in every language. I remember reading an interview with a Swedish illustrator who was asked 'When did you start drawing?', and his answer to the interviewer was 'When did you stop?'

I came to illustration by an unusual route. I began college as a mechanical engineering student in Manchester.... My limited attention span forced me to sit at the back of the lectures, reading Viz and drawing puerile caricatures of the lecturers and unpopular students with a biro on lined paper. Luckily, in my first student house there were two really talented illustration students, and I started hanging around with them, I bought a sketchbook and a pencil, and the rest is history. I never got bored drawing pictures, it was perfectly suited to all of my failings and personality traits. I liked that every drawing was unique, and that there were considerably more girls studying illustration than engineering.

I think clients use me for what happens in between my ears as much as what happens at the end of my fingers. To communicate visually, I try to combine and subvert visual cliché, I like to use humour where it is appropriate. My work has evolved to allow me to work to very tight deadlines – often under five hours. My shortest deadline was twenty minutes! Intense concentration, ability to hyper-focus for short periods...ability to make decisions and communicate under pressure.

I suspect that the parts of my brain that I use when I draw have grown or optimized to enable me to work more efficiently. Editorial illustration is just professional Pictionary really, without friends and alcohol. When a client sends an editorial commission, I will grab a pencil, open my sketchbook and read the text. My head is filled with random imagery and concepts as I read the article, and I make quick thumbnail sketches as I read.

I don't know whether this has always happened, or if this has developed with experience, but the best ideas tend to resonate in my head – like a tuning fork will resonate when placed next to a note of the right frequency. I will describe the biggest 'hum' as the 'main concept'. I use this as a framework for the illustration. I can fine-tune, subvert and wrap other concepts into the framework to make the final illustration. I play with it until the deadline, and/or/if everyone is happy.

In November 2015, I did a job for the Guardian newspaper sports pages, illustrating an article about the apparent proliferation of brain damage in retired professional footballers. The journalist referred to medical research linking the small, repeated impacts of heading a football to incidents of brain injury in retired players.

A Newton's Cradle is a 1980s executive toy. When a sphere at one end is lifted and

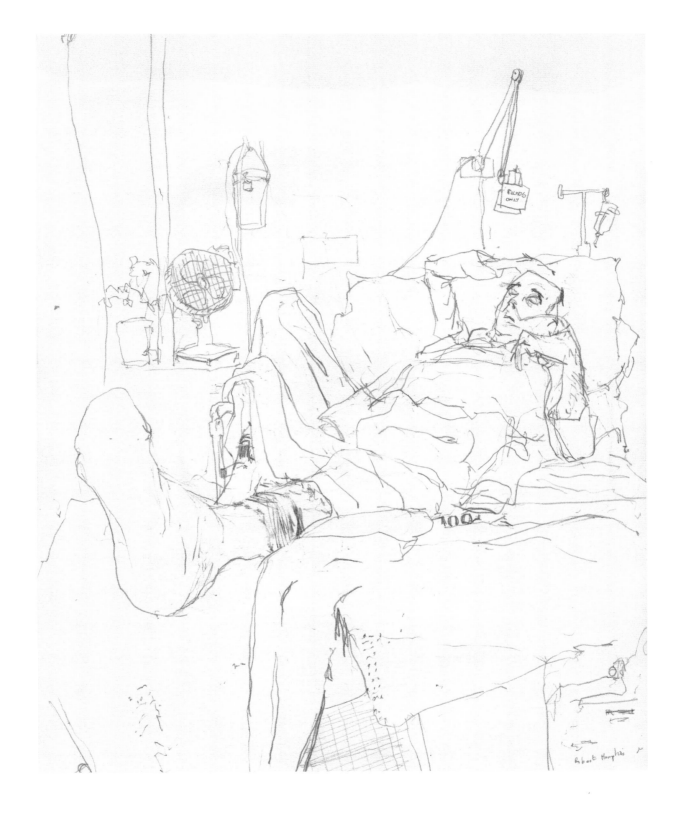

Above: One of the numerous observational drawings David Humphries made during the many hours he spent by his father's hospital bedside. The drawings are moving in their intimacy.

David Humphries

Drawing and Applied Illustration

released, it strikes the stationary spheres, transmitting a force through the stationary spheres that pushes the last sphere upwards. It hummed loudly in my head because:

1. It is perfect for describing small repeated impacts over a long period of time.
2. It was the right shape for the design format (landscape).
3. It has spheres that I could change into footballs.

I particularly liked the concept because the footballer would not be able to stop heading the ball – the energy and momentum of the Newton's Cradle would create endless impacts. I usually grab references from the internet to help me to compose the image into the allocated space. Here, I added a footballer in a 'diving header' position. The West Bromwich Albion kit is a reference to Jeff Astle, whose brain damage was highlighted in this context. I tried to turn the Cradle's frame into goal posts and add the netting, but these ideas detracted from the main concept. Played with it until 5.30 p.m. Sent artwork. Went to the pub.

I primarily consider drawing as visual communication. Sometimes it is easy to forget that every drawing starts as a blank piece of paper or an empty computer screen. Whereas thinking of an idea is like panning for gold, it feels more like alchemy when I create a collection of marks and shapes that communicates or entertains.

I have always found it difficult to mentally bridge the chasm between my figurative drawing and my professional work; they do different things. I have always been pragmatic, and conceptual imagery often requires a graphic element that is absent in observational drawing, though the skills involved are not mutually exclusive.

My illustration has always been shaped-based. Shapes enable me to work quickly and efficiently. I like shapes; it may be the way I look at things, or the way I think or make sense of the world. I create my illustrations in Photoshop using a Wacom tablet. I use the lasso tool a lot, it is very similar to drawing shapes with a pencil. Large, simple shapes are ideally suited to short editorial deadlines, and they produce bold images that print well. I am not sure whether I was attracted to editorial illustration because of the way I work, or my work is a symptom of editorial illustration.

Some of the most creative people I know are not artists. I have always loved making and fixing things. I inherited this from my dad, who understood how things work. I believe that this innate curiosity is linked to creativity. These people can always draw – simple diagrams that 'work' – and this ability can be developed and honed. It is impossible to draw a bike from memory unless you understand how it works.

When I was a student, I remember visiting an exhibition of drawings at the Royal College of Art by Sir Isaac Newton and his contemporaries. I was really annoyed that all of the scientists could draw better than me. After the exhibition, when I was sitting under a tree in Hyde Park, an iPhone dropped out of the sky and hit me on the head. At that moment it occurred to me that very few modern illustrators have the technical ability to make drawings of that quality, and it is the advent of photography that has allowed drawing to disappear from the science curriculum (and the majority of art schools). But the real loss is that the act (and discipline) of describing things visually helps us to understand their function and appreciate their beauty; merely pressing a button on a camera or a phone just isn't the same.

Opposite and above: Various editorial commissions undertaken by David Humphries.
Following spread: The impactful 'Newton's Cradle' illustration for a *Guardian* newspaper article about the increasing incidence of brain injury in retired footballers.

David Humphries

Book illustration

'The best illustration in this field is careful to avoid duplicating or visualizing literally the writer's words. Often a more tangential approach is required, suggesting mood, background or atmosphere'

The use of illustration for adult fiction, as distinct from young adult fiction, children's book illustration or picturebook-making, is perhaps less common than it was in the past and tends to be confined primarily to publishers of lavishly designed and produced collectable editions such as the Folio Society in the UK and the Limited Editions Club in the US. That said, in recent years book design and production generally has seen a noticeable surge in print and production quality, with commercial books of all categories needing to become much more desirable as objects in order to compete with screen-based reading. Non-fiction hardback books in particular have made increasing use of illustration, especially in fields such as nature writing, lifestyle and travel, where book cover and jacket design especially have once again become boom areas for illustrators.

Illustration for fiction can be a contentious area. Commissioning an artist to add pictorial interpretations to a text that was originally conceived and written as a stand-alone experience is not always welcome. Writers and readers can sometimes feel that illustration intrudes on the reader's imagination. But the best illustration in this field is careful to avoid duplicating or visualizing literally the writer's words. Often a more tangential approach

is required, suggesting mood, background or atmosphere, creating a counterpoint to the reading of words and augmenting the overall aesthetic experience. Ardizzone touched on these issues in another rare excursion into analysis in issue 11 of *ARK*, the iconic journal of the Royal College of Art, in 1954:

> *The Function of an Illustrator: The illustrator has to add to the work of the author. He has to explain something to the reader which the author cannot say in words or has not the space to do so. His illustrations should form an evocative visual background to the story, a background which the reader can people with the characters of the author. The suggestion and the hint are often more important than the clear-cut statement. Don't do too much of the reader's work for him; rather, help him to use his imagination. Be careful of the dramatic scenes in a book. Violence and drama are often better expressed in words. It is easy to fall into the trap of being literary. The approach to illustration should be purely visual.*

OPPOSITE: Edward McKnight Kauffer's illustrations for Arnold Bennett's *Elsie and the Child* (Cassell, 1929) were produced using the technique of pochoir – stencils designed by the artist and hand-coloured at the Curwen Press.

Evelyn Dunbar
Lyrical non-fiction

The British painter and illustrator Evelyn Dunbar is perhaps best known for her paintings as an official war artist, in particular depicting the activities of the Women's Land Army during the Second World War. In 1938, the publisher Noel Carrington, a great supporter and promoter of artists whose work he admired, invited Dunbar to illustrate the new edition of A Gardener's Diary, the previous edition of which had been illustrated by Edward Bawden. Carrington was responsible for commissioning young talents such as Eric Ravilious, Bawden and Kathleen Hale through his work as editor at the publication Country Life and his development of the highly successful Puffin Picture Books. Dunbar produced lyrical, expressive line drawings of working figures for the tailpieces of A Gardener's Diary, rendered in simple line and informed by her love of gardening and the countryside.

In 2013, a batch of preparatory studies, along with a treasure trove of other work by the artist, was discovered. Often the preparatory sketches and working drawings of illustrators in the past were discarded, as indeed was the final artwork for reproduction, which was often seen as serving no further purpose after it had been photographed for reproduction. One particularly distressing story saw a substantial body of original work by a highly respected twentieth-century illustrator being rescued from a rubbish skip after her death; fortunately, it is now cared for at Seven Stories, the National Centre for Children's Books in Newcastle, UK. There is now growing awareness of the importance of looking after original artwork and preparatory studies for published illustration. This is all the more important at a time when a great deal of published illustration is produced wholly or partially through digital media, thereby leaving little or no trace of process.

Dunbar's illustrations for A Gardener's Diary, and the various sketches and experimental drawings that went into their making, give a clear sense of an artist bringing personal expertise in a subject, allied to a lyrical, poetic painter's eye, to a relatively humble commercial non-fiction project. The crossover between her work as painter and illustrator is seamless. Some of the motifs used in the book illustrations were later worked up into paintings or recycled in different forms in other projects. The more worked-up illustration studies in ink retain the pencil underdrawing.

Above: A preparatory drawing by Evelyn Dunbar for the title page of
A *Gardener's Diary*, showing the pencil underdrawing (*Country Life*, 1938).
Following page, above: A selection of small drop-in line illustrations for
A *Farm Dictionary* (Evans, 1953).
Following page, below: A sheet of studies for Evelyn Dunbar's Brockley School mural.
p. 161, above: Artwork for the title page of *Gardeners' Choice*, showing pencil
underdrawing and notes to the printer.
p. 161, below: Printed title page for A *Gardener's Diary*.

Evelyn Dunbar

SEED-BARROW

LEAN-TO

RAVE

Drawing and Applied Illustration

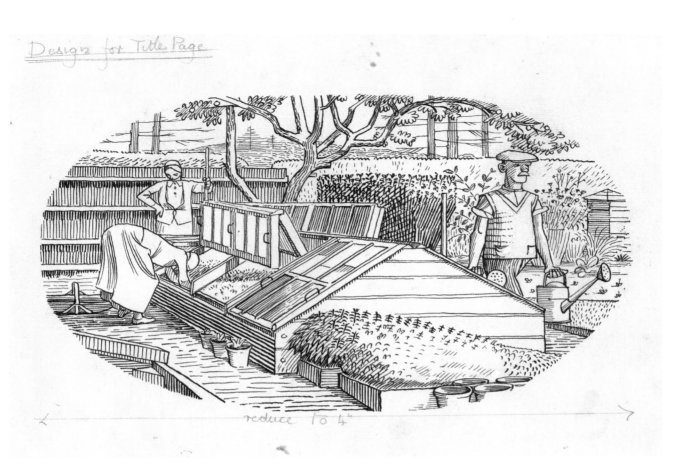

Design for Title Page

reduce to 4"

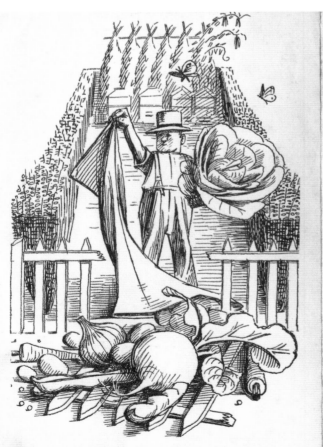

A GARDENER'S
DIARY
1938

Designed by
EVELYN DUNBAR

London:
Published by
COUNTRY LIFE

136 PAGES ILLUSTRATED   THE SIZE OF THIS PROSPECTUS   2s. 6d. NET

Evelyn Dunbar

Pablo Auladell
La Feria Abandonada

Working across comics and illustration, and 'sometimes even blurring the boundaries between those two languages', the Spanish artist Pablo Auladell has received several major awards for his lyrical, dream-like illustration that is deeply rooted in classical, expressive draughtsmanship. His prolific output reaches over seventy books, working with a range of authors and texts, contemporary and classic, as well as his own authorial projects. He also finds time to teach at the *Ars in Fabula* School of Illustration in Macerata, Italy. In 2016, his graphic novel version of Milton's *Paradise Lost* was published in English by Jonathan Cape.

La Feria Abandonada (The Abandoned Carnival), published by Barbara Fiore in 2013, began life as a visual idea that ultimately required Auladell to commission writers to provide complementary words to this essentially visual concept. Ardizzone's assertion that the function of the illustrator is 'to add to the work of the author' is here turned on its head, with the writers being commissioned to 'explain something to the reader which the author cannot say in pictures or has not the space to do so'. The outline concept had been in Auladell's mind and in his sketchbooks for

some time, but he decided to seek the help of two writer friends, journalist Rafa Burgos and poet Julián López Medina, to, in his own words 'enrich' the project. Projects such as this, where the artist's vision is the driving force behind a book, are an increasingly significant part of the illustration landscape.

Auladell's artworks are 'drawn' directly on paper, and his thoughts on the processes involved in the production of the book, his range of visual and textual references and search for new directions in visual language are expressed as lyrically and poetically as the images themselves:

The first thing that comes to me is the name, the title of the project, and then a vision, an image that appears more or less clearly in my mind and becomes a sort of atmospheric, aesthetic pattern. The name of the project, the name of the book is essential for me when I begin a work that has not been commissioned. The genetic code of the whole artwork is there as if it were an egg. It has deep implications, the musicality of its sound, the rhythm, the tempo – a series of evocations, a lighthouse which points the way to follow. All this means that in the first stages, I draw very little and think a lot.

I soon realized that the carnival I was interested in creating for the illustrations must not be a 'Tod Browning carnival'. It is not a freak book. Its texts don't tell stories of humiliation or social exclusion, but sing of a world that is disappearing, the world that people in my age group had known. These texts try to take a photograph of the place where we were happy, where we lived through something important, but a world now without us. So I began to look for models with a poetic sense that was closer to that of Solana, Picasso, Varela....

For La Feria Abandonada, I was at that time working hard on changing my iconography and trying to incorporate a more Mediterranean, archaic (in the sense of an image out of time, where time has been suspended) graphic tradition that was 'closer to me'. So, you could say that this book is the first canon of that new way of drawing, which I have been developing further since then, making adjustments after every picture-book, failing and solving graphic problems, a never-ending process because it consists of improving a tool, sharpening a knife in order to make a deeper wound, tuning up in order to sing better.

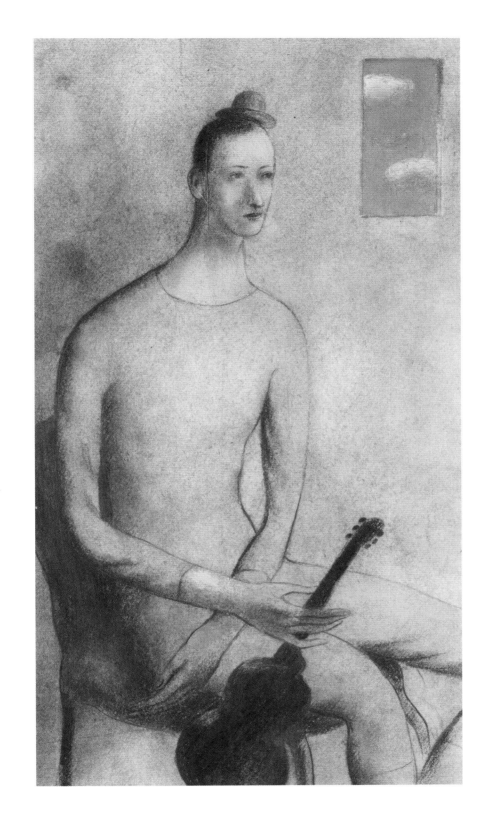

Above: The first 'vision' drawing that Pablo Auladell made when setting out on the creative journey of making *La Feria Abandonada*.
Following spread: Some of Auladell's very early sketches for *La feria*.
pp. 166–67: A final spread from *La Feria Abandonada* (texts by Rafa Burgos and Julián López Medina, Barbara Fiore, 2013).

Pablo Auladell

Drawing and Applied Illustration

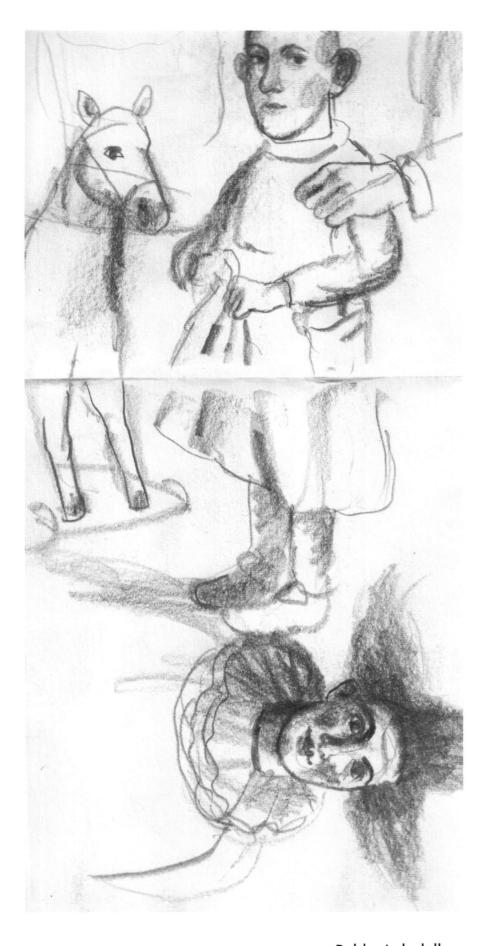

All the prior work of preparing the final artwork is made in sketchbooks, but the point is not to draw preparatory sketches for specific images of the final book. If I draw in this way, the final picture will become dead. I always draw 'alla prima' because, if not, I feel that I prefer the first sketch to the final picture. I clearly feel that something important, essential and mysterious has been lost in the process.

So I work like a sportsman, warming up before the jump, drawing a lot, trying to enter and capture the particular atmosphere, the gestures and drama of the characters. When I feel I am fully immersed in this particular world, I try a first image, usually that one that I mentioned at the beginning that appears in my mind as the first vision. If I fail, I try again. But always working 'alla prima'.

When I finally get that first image to the stage of being a finished picture, all the subsequent work builds on this discipline, on drawing that is so concentrated on the laws hidden in that picture. This is the point that destroys that stupid belief about 'artistic freedom'. Although I am working on my own project and nobody has told me what to do or how to draw, how to make the 'proper' picture you are drawing, it is now the book I am building that is telling me what is required. So perhaps we can say that drawing is a long process of learning to become capable of listening to what your artwork is demanding and what it is refusing.

Pablo Auladell

Drawing and Applied Illustration

Pablo Auladell

Character development

'It is often only when two or more characters are drawn interacting with each other that they really begin to assert their respective identities'

For illustrators working in the field of children's books, especially picturebook-making, the creation of convincing and consistent characters is particularly important. To create characters that are absolutely believable normally demands a great deal of time spent in the sketchbook or on endless sheets of paper. Sometimes the artist may have a very clear idea in mind as to the key personality traits of the character(s), while sometimes the characters may only really assert themselves (and perhaps surprise their creator) on paper, as the drawing grows in confidence.

Whichever way around the process works, it is often only when two or more characters are drawn interacting with each other that they really begin to assert their respective identities and eventually start to dictate the development of a narrative. This is a process that I liken to the gradual maturation of a TV drama series or situation comedy. Many writers for television series have spoken of how early episodes come to be looked back on as somewhat stilted and forced, as the actors try to make sense of their roles. After a period of time, they begin to better know their characters' identities and start to 'add on' various mannerisms and idiosyncrasies to their roles. The writers in turn find themselves 'writing for the characters' as the actors increasingly contribute to establishing their identities. Consequently, the nature of the 'situations' that are written into the situation comedy are increasingly led by the dramatic possibilities that interactions between the contrasting personalities present.

OPPOSITE: Early character studies by Axel Scheffler for the almost universally popular Gruffalo, a character invented by the English writer Julia Donaldson in the mid-1990s.

Fifi Kuo and Ellie Snowdon Approaches to animal character

Two illustrator–authors whose approaches to character design and development are rooted respectively in their own particular approaches to drawing are Fifi Kuo and Ellie Snowdon. Although each has a solid grounding in observational drawing, Kuo can be seen as an example of an artist whose characters emerge 'from within', driven in the first instance by her emotions and motivations. Snowdon comes from a background of keen interest in natural history and consequent experience of drawing animals directly from observation. Both of them developed the characters shown here while studying as students.

Fifi Kuo is an illustrator from Taiwan whose picturebooks are becoming increasingly familiar in the English-speaking world as well as in numerous other languages and territories. Her success is rooted in the utterly convincing characters that emerge from her sketchbooks. It is within these pages that their personalities are 'written' in pictures, through a process of drawing and more drawing.

The characters Panda and Penguin first appeared in a very quickly sketched two-frame sequence in Kuo's student sketchbook.

Panda sits working at a laptop, Penguin brings a hot drink. Although this would not seem to be the most enticing starting point for possible full-length picturebooks, there is a whole world of empathy in these two frames, a deep bond between the two of them that is subtly, visually evident. The two characters are then taken on various outings within the pages of the sketchbook to explore how they interact. It is never evident what gender they are, whether they are children or adults, or even the nature of their relationship. But they are utterly convincing as they go about their business. We are hooked. We care what happens to them because their creator clearly does. They embody friendship, warmth and empathy.

By contrast, Ellie Snowdon's personal project to illustrate *The Owl and the Pussycat* in picturebook form gives us a glimpse of the extent and depth of formal research that can often be necessary when developing convincing animal characters from scratch and putting them through complex anthropomorphized movements. While Kuo's approach could be said to be partly intuitive, Snowdon's

approach is systematic and methodical. Her longstanding interest in natural history helps her to draw animals and birds convincingly, but taking naturalistic observation and developing it into imaginative character drawing requires a series of careful adjustments through extensive experimental drawing. Adapting the anatomy of animals and birds to those of humans demands considerable levels of understanding of both. The challenges involved in drawing an owl and a pussycat dancing closely together are considerable. Snowdon first studied videos of human dancers, making numerous drawings to closely examine their movements and the ways in which they interact. The next stage involved a process of testing through drawing the extent to which the vastly different anatomies could be reconfigured, to allow for the suggestion of convincingly syncopated movements and gestures from these alien creatures. Many liberties needed to be taken with relative scale, and occasionally limbs and joints, yet the characters somehow remain essentially true to their zoological origins.

Above: Fifi Kuo's picturebook *The Perfect Sofa* (Boxer Books, 2019) features the characters Panda and Penguin situated in a domestic, human environment, trying to decide on a new sofa.

Fifi Kuo and Ellie Snowdon

Pages from Kuo's sketchbook showing the development of an
idea for the first Panda and Penguin story, including visual notes
on narrative moments, sequence and pace, and colour schemes.

Drawing and Applied Illustration

Fifi Kuo's two characters, Panda and Penguin, are very naturally integrated
into the landscapes that they find themselves in. Even when dwarfed
by their surroundings, the deep bond between them is evident.

Fifi Kuo and Ellie Snowdon

Above and opposite: Examples of some of the many stages involved in Snowdon's quest to achieve convincing representation of the anthropomorphic Owl and Pussycat.

Drawing and Applied Illustration

Fifi Kuo and Ellie Snowdon

Axel Scheffler
The evolution of a personal visual vocabulary

There are not many illustrators who can lay claim to the term 'household name', but the creator of the visual representation of Julia Donaldson's ubiquitous *Gruffalo* is certainly one. Although he has illustrated somewhere in the region of 150 books, and worked variously on concepts of his own, group projects that he has organized for a range of causes and his 'artists' books', published in Germany, it is for his part in the global phenomenon of *The Gruffalo* that Axel Scheffler is inevitably best known.

After discovering that he didn't want to continue studying Art History in Hamburg, Axel Scheffler first came to the UK in the early 1980s to study Illustration at Bath Academy of Art (now part of Bath Spa University), where he was encouraged to draw from observation:

I think I had done a little bit of observational drawing, but really I think that only happened properly when I went to art school and people told me that that was what I had to do. You know – 'keep a sketchbook and draw from life', that sort of thing.

The course at Bath had a relationship with the historic School of Art at Cooper Union in New York City, and Scheffler was able to spend three months drawing there on an exchange. It seems clear that the stylistic robustness of his chunky characters had its foundations there, in the heavy, muscular pencil work of his drawings. But he finds it difficult to see:

In my case I find it quite hard to make a connection between what I did as a student and observational drawings and my work. I think it's an entirely different way of drawing, I am basically making things up. I don't think any of my sketching and observational drawing fed into my professional work...unless subconsciously, that's always a possibility. When I'm illustrating a story by Julia Donaldson I often think perhaps I should look at trees and things. Of course, the more you do the more you get better, or more confident but I can't see myself building up a skill to make picturebooks by sketching or observational drawings. They were separate areas of drawing for me.

I longed to learn something or to be taught something, really, but I didn't get that. I am all for the academic drawing and life

drawing and all that. I think that's a good thing for anyone. But I can't really see how it fed into my picturebook work. It's just sort of 'made up' images really. I'm not, as I always say, a very 'skilful' draughtsman or someone who can 'draw correctly' but somehow it works. Well, it works within the world of picturebooks, which have their own logic...so it doesn't really matter whether hands look like hands or cows look like cows. Although I don't think I learned much at art college, the experience of drawing for three years and trying things out I think was important. So I wouldn't say I didn't need to go to art college, but I feel very much that my 'technique' or my way of doing picturebooks – that was self-taught.

But everyone is different, and everyone finds their own way. It's hard to unravel or deconstruct how that is arrived at or what makes a 'style'. There is a connection from my student days, of course, because I did a lot of editorial work – in a kind of cartoony style with big pointy noses. I think for the picturebooks, when I first drew, for example, A Squash and a Squeeze with Julia Donaldson,

Top: A rough colour page layout by Axel Scheffler for the global publishing
phenomenon *The Gruffalo* (text by Julia Donaldson, MacMillan Children's Books, 1999).
Above: Early incarnations of the Gruffalo were seen by the publishing team as a
little too malevolent-looking for the reader age.
Following spread: An early sheet of character studies for *The Gruffalo*.

Axel Scheffler

I drew the little old lady with a very pointy nose and sagging breasts, but the publishers pushed me in another direction – they wanted her to be round and cute. And so I compromised. I'm sure my picturebook style could have taken a completely different direction if I had had more artistic freedom...making compromises with the commercial world, that's what started it and I just carried on in that direction. I wasn't allowed to draw people for a long time because of the noses, but eventually I reached a stage where Macmillan, my publisher, said 'you're allowed to do noses'. I find it hard to analyse but I clearly made compromises towards the expectations of the publishers – or the market, who knows, from early on, and it was a direction that I took, perhaps neglecting some aspects of what I had in 'freer' work.

With The Gruffalo, again, the publishers pushed me in a certain direction. I started sketching the Gruffalo looking more scary than he did in the end. The publishers said, 'Let's have him less scary and more lovable'. They were probably right. I meet some people now who say that their child can't sleep when The Gruffalo book is in the room. Although children like to be scared, I think it can be too much. When people ask me what's the secret behind the success of The Gruffalo I often think it's to do with the ambiguity between him being threatening, not 'evil' but hungry, and on the other hand being quite stupid. And some children find him even quite cuddly or sweet. So that's part of the appeal of the book. If he was just scary then I think the book wouldn't have been such a success.

Drawing and Applied Illustration

Atmosphere
and fantasy

'The richly illustrated "gift book" fantasies
by the likes of Rackham and Dulac during the
late Victorian period have exerted a lasting
influence on imaginative book illustration'

The last decades of the nineteenth century and the first two decades of the twentieth were a Golden Age for illustration. New possibilities in full-colour printing emerged, precipitating an explosion of sumptuous and imaginative watercolour illustration by the likes of Arthur Rackham, Kay Nielsen and Edmund Dulac in Europe, while in America the growth in popular magazines saw many respected figurative artists, including John Sloan and William Glackens, become regular and greatly admired contributors to popular publications. The richly illustrated 'gift book' fantasies by the likes of Rackham and Dulac during the late Victorian period have exerted a lasting influence on imaginative book illustration.

The world of fairies and wonderlands continues to engage and enthrall, and is kept alive today through the combined vision and watercolour craftsmanship of artists such as Alan Lee and P. J. Lynch. It is perhaps true to say that the convincing visualization of fantastic worlds and mystical, mythical creatures can be at its most effective when represented in an essentially realist, idiomatic manner. Making the unreal real, if you will, demands great technical skill as well as vision.

OPPOSITE: 'At this the whole pack rose up into the air, and came flying down upon her.' During what has come to be known as the Golden Age of illustration, Lewis Carroll's *Alice's Adventures in Wonderland* (1865) came into the public domain and precipitated the publication of many new illustrated editions. Arthur Rackham's 1907 version for William Heinemann is perhaps the best remembered.

Atmosphere and fantasy

'I'm very bad at keeping sketchbooks, but I do try to keep a record
of experiences from everyday life, fragments of memory, characters,
thoughts, feelings, quotes or anything that moves me'

Victoria Turnbull
Authorial flights of fancy

Victoria Turnbull's illustration work is notable for its exceptional level of craftsmanship and painstaking rendering. Her picturebooks can be compared to operatic productions, each page like a carefully designed stage set, every inch filled with voluptuous detail. Her authorship of these books is almost entirely visual, with minimum levels of supporting text. Her work reveals an intuitive approach that is not based on formal observational drawing, but is nevertheless rooted in the observation of people and nature.

Observation
Drawing is a way for me to communicate with my unconscious, to generate ideas and to give physical form to the things in my head. My drawing has always been a bridge to the imagination. Like a great many children, my love for drawing began when I was very young. If I wasn't drawing from my imagination, I would be meticulously copying pictures I found in books or on television (I would record on a VCR and pause the video to draw fuzzy stills of cartoon characters). This compulsive childhood drawing is the foundation of my illustration work today.

I did not, and still do not particularly enjoy drawing from life (much of my observational drawing experience has been in an educational setting). That isn't to say I don't recognize the importance of observation to drawing. I think an interest in and a curiosity about the world is essential for an illustrator. When I do draw from life, my gaze tends to be pulled by the human subject or to the natural world and not by inanimate manmade objects. I'm very bad at keeping sketchbooks, but I do try to keep a record of experiences from everyday life, fragments of memory, characters, thoughts, feelings, quotes or anything that moves me. I enjoy the merging of fact and fiction on the page. I find connections emerge between these random notes and doodles and stories begin to form.

Much of my drawing is based on intuition. I try to draw from inside myself. I will draw something over and over until it looks right and feels true to my experience. By referencing the world we share, I hope my imaginary drawings seem more real and come alive for the reader. The characters in my stories take shape through the process of drawing. They develop into personalities I feel I know. The illustrators I most admire are those that draw with empathy and are able to externalize the inner emotions of a character. This is always my ambition when it comes to my own work. I wish to establish an emotional connection with the reader that will, in some small way, colour their experience of the world.

Process and technique
My initial drawings are drawn on tracing paper in pencil. I enjoy the smooth texture of tracing paper and the ability to layer one image over another (it also avoids the very real prospect of ruining expensive paper with terrible drawings). I scan my pencil drawings and scale them, to preserve the integrity of the line, before printing them out onto high quality paper. I then colour the printed pencil images with a mixture of pastel and coloured pencil, sometimes blending areas with linseed oil or highlighting with gouache. After scanning the coloured artwork, I'll use Photoshop to make any corrections and to add a little 'oomph' to the colour.

Above: Victoria Turnbull's technique of working in pencil on tracing paper before printing and adding colour was developed through trial and error when working on what would become her debut picturebook, *The Sea Tiger* (Templar, 2014), while studying for her MA degree.

Victoria Turnbull

Controlling tone and colour

My first book was developed in the final stages of my MA course. I drew the initial sketches for **The Sea Tiger** in pencil without considering how I would add the colour, because at that time I didn't have a particular process, I just wanted to get the drawings right. As a result I shaded in large areas of the drawings so they worked in black and white, but there was simply too much tone for them to work successfully as colour illustrations. I had to carefully remove large areas of pencil and redraw sections so I could use them for the final artwork.

I feel comfortable using a pencil but colour is something I've had to work very hard at. Finding a good balance between drawing and colour is often trial and error, as it can be difficult to recognize mid-process. With experience this has got easier but sometimes I'm so intent on making a beautiful drawing that I get carried away and add too much pencil. I draw on tracing paper, and I have learned to add large areas of tone to the reverse so that it's easier to remove and make adjustments where necessary.

Above: Pencil sketch and finished artwork
for *Pandora* (Frances Lincoln, 2016).

Drawing and Applied Illustration

Above: A very simple compositional sketch shown above an intricately crafted final spread from *Cloud Forest* (Lincoln Children's Books, 2019).

Victoria Turnbull

Sheila Robinson
The Twelve Dancing Princesses

Born in Nottingham, UK, Sheila Robinson was one of a group of mid-twentieth century artist–illustrators who settled in the English village of Great Bardfield, and subsequently became known as the Great Bardfield Group. Like Edward Bawden and Eric Ravilious, who were seen as the leading lights of this group, she worked comfortably across the fine and applied arts throughout the 1950s and 1960s, taking on such varied commissions as designing an ark of animals for a seaside fairground ride, assisting Bawden in the production of a mural for the 1951 Festival of Britain and creating a series of card-print illustrations for a deluxe edition of D. H. Lawrence's *Sons and Lovers* for the Limited Editions Club of New York. Her illustrative work was published widely in books and magazines of the period.

An early self-initiated project to design and illustrate one of the traditional German tales collected by the Brothers Grimm, *The Twelve Dancing Princesses*, was developed into a completely hand-rendered dummy book that now resides at the Fry Art Gallery and Museum in Essex, where a collection of the work of the Great Bardfield Group is held. This exquisitely rendered dummy book is the product of extensive visual research that we are able to study thanks to the accompanying research sketchbook.

The preservation of a sketchbook such as this gives us a particularly acute insight into the depth and breadth of research or 'drawing for illustration' that underpins the development of what is often casually referred to as an artist's 'style'. Robinson's exploratory work includes costume reference studies, drawn from observation at the Victoria and Albert Museum in London, general background drawing and experimentation with various media and detailed rough page designs for the final artworks, vigorously sketched in black and white with accompanying handwritten text. The hand-stitched dummy book was created to the format of the Puffin Picture Books series, conceived by Noel Carrington and Allen Lane at Penguin in the 1940s, which became a hugely successful series through into the early 1970s. The landscape-format books alternated full-colour and black and white spreads and could be printed on one very large sheet of paper, colour on one side, black and white on the other. The single sheet was then folded and cut into a thirty-two-page book, making it very cheap to produce. A facsimile version of this book was published in 2012 at Anglia Ruskin University.

Robinson's daughter, Chloë Cheese, herself a leading illustrator and printmaker, tells us all she can about her late mother's unpublished project:

The story behind The Twelve Dancing Princesses *seems to be that my mother drew it during her time at Nottingham (as there is a reference to it in a letter from a friend, asking if she had had any luck with it, implying that it had been seen in Nottingham, although the letter is addressed to Sheila at the Royal College of Art). But she had no luck with publication as that particular series had been stopped. Being preoccupied with other things, my mother never tried again. Much later, the writer Olive Cook was also very taken with it, but she had no luck either. The ability to make digital changes to spelling mistakes was really helpful to its final publication through the university. My mother did not persevere after rejection with any of her work, as she was too proud and always took the rejections quite deeply to heart. The publication at Anglia Ruskin University with Brian Webb's design was lovely though, and I do feel sorry that my mother did not have the heart-warming experience of a later appreciation of all her work.*

I loved being read the story from Sheila's original when I was little, and definitely appreciated it myself.

1875.

Thune Toilet of black faille

The train skirt has a coquillé of bows of black ribbon carried up the centre. The outer edge of the train is trimm'd with a flounce with bouillonné above. drawn bands of faille are placed crosswise between the flounces & the coquillé. the Tablier is full & trimmed with 3 rows of deep fringe. the sleeves are drawn with straps of faille crossing them at intervals

163.

Above: Sheila Robinson's research for *The Twelve Dancing Princesses* took
her to the Victoria and Albert Museum in London to sketch period costumes.
Following spread: Sheila Robinson's 1950s research sketchbook for her self-initiated
project to create a picturebook version of *The Twelve Dancing Princesses*. The unselfconscious
functionality of these intense studies makes them exquisitely compelling in themselves.
pp. 190–91: A finished spread from *The Twelve Dancing Princesses*.

Sheila Robinson

As he was about to go to bed, the eldest Princess appeared bringing him a cup of wine, but he had fastened a sponge under his chin and let the wine run down into it, so that he did not drink one drop. Then he lay down and when he had been quiet a little while he began to snore as though in the deepest sleep.

The twelve princesses heard him and laughed. The eldest said "He could fall asleep like the rest." Then they got out of bed, opened cupboards chests and cases, and brought out their beautiful dresses & decked themselves before the glass skipping about and rejoicing in the prospect of the dance.

But the youngest sister said "I don't know what it is. You may rejoice but I feel as if a strange misfortune is certainly hanging over us." "You are a little goose," answered the eldest, "you are always frightened. Have you forgotten how many princes have come here in vain? I had need not have given the soldier a sleeping draught. I'll wager the blockhead would never have awakened."

When they were all ready they looked at the soldier but his eyes were shut and he did not stir. So they thought they would soon be quite safe. Then the eldest went up to one of the beds and knocked on it, it sank into the earth and they descended through the opening one after another, the eldest first.

They went on farther and came to a great lake close to the bank lay twelve little boats, and in every boat sat a handsome Prince, they had expected the twelve Princesses and each took one with him.

but the Soldier seated himself by the youngest. But then said the Prince "I don't know why, but the boat is much heavier today and I am obliged to row with all my strength if I can't sail." "I wonder why" said the youngest unless perhaps it is the hot weather, I am uncommonly hot"

On the opposite side of the lake stood a splendid brightly light castle, from which came the sound of the joyous music of trumpets and drums.

The next morning the
soldier determined,
to say nothing but
to see the wonderful
doings again. So
he went with them
the second and
third nights.
Everything was
just the same
as the first time
and they danced
even some till
their shoes were
in holes, but
the third time
the Soldier took
away with him a
wine cup as a token.

be in
be
fir...

When the
appointed
hour came
for his answer
he took the
three twigs
and the cup
with him and
went before
the King.

The twelve princesses stood behind the
door listening to hear what he would
say. So the King put the Question
Where did my daughters dance their
shoes to pieces in the night. he answered
With twelve Princes in a beautiful
underground castle. Then he produced
the Token, the three twigs one of silver
one gold and one of diamonds. also
cup which he had taken the last night.

there upon the King
asked the Soldier
which one he would
chose as his wife.
He answered, I am
no longer young,
give me the eldest.
So the wedding
was celebrated that
very day, and
the Kingdom was
promised to the
Soldier on the King's
death... but for
every night the Princes
had spent in dancing
with the Princesses as
many years were added to
their enchantment
and lived happily ever after.

THE TWELVE DANCING
PRINCESSES
A Grimm Fairy Tale
with drawings by Gordon King

DRINCE
A Grimm Fairy Tale
with a
drawings

On the opposite side of the lake stood a splendid brightly lit castle

...from which came the sound of the joyous music of trumpet and drums.

Authorial graphic storytelling

'Many illustrators now see it as the ultimate creative field to aspire to'

The role and identity of the illustrator continues to evolve, broaden and, increasingly, embrace authorship. Comics and graphic novels are gradually being accorded greater respect as an important branch of literature. Reviews in mainstream literary publications display a growing acceptance and understanding of this fusion of art, design and literature, and there is a noticeable growth in the confidence of reviewers to find a vocabulary with which to appraise their subjects. Children's picturebook-makers, too, have seen an explosion of interest in their authorship. In marked contrast to the situation twenty or thirty years ago, when this area of work received little serious attention in art schools, many illustrators now see it as the ultimate creative field to which to aspire.

In both picturebook-making and graphic storytelling, the author is responsible for all aspects of this multimodal medium in a way that is perhaps comparable to the singer-songwriter who composes a song, sings it and plays all of the instruments in their own recording studio. There are obvious ways in which draughtsmanship forms a basis for this process, just as musicianship does in the above analogy. But it also plays a key role in research and information-gathering, page layout and character design.

OPPOSITE: One of the most influential artists in the development of authorial graphic narrative was Winsor McCay. His *Little Nemo in Slumberland* ran from October 1905 to July 1911 in the *New York Herald*, and to 1927 in other publications. In this September 1907 strip, Little Nemo and Little Imp become giants and explore the city.

Authorial graphic storytelling

'Drawing from observation has been hugely important to my work... drawing on location was integral to my process'

Isabel Greenberg
Glass Town

Isabel Greenberg has emerged in recent years as one of the most original, intelligent and imaginative graphic authors working in the genre. *Glass Town* was published by Jonathan Cape to great acclaim in early 2020. The book takes the Brontë siblings' early immersion in their fantasy worlds of Angria, Gondal and Glass Town, and, as James Smart put it in his 2020 review in the *Guardian* newspaper, 'blurs fiction and memoir: characters walk between worlds and woo their creators'. It is perhaps unsurprising that Greenberg found it difficult to choose between art school and a more traditionally 'academic' education that would accommodate her passion for literature and history. All of these interests are evident in *Glass Town*. As a child, her family were happy to encourage her to draw:

My parents worked together running a company that designed exhibitions, so they were very supportive of me pursuing a creative path. It would probably have been very surprising to them if I had become a doctor or something – which I hasten to say was never an option in terms of the necessary skills!

In terms of going on to higher education, at seventeen every decision, even choosing a sandwich, seemed huge and potentially life-changing to me. I loved English and History at school just as much as I loved Art, so university versus art school was a decision I went back and forth on a lot. Looking back, I know there are a lot of things I missed that I would have hugely enjoyed in a more academic education, but in terms of the life path my choice set me on, I have no regrets at all.

Drawing from observation has been hugely important to my work. My book projects tend to be quite long-form and research-heavy anyway, but for Glass Town, drawing on location was integral to my process. While you can see a flat rendering of a place from a photo, the atmosphere and the smell and the sounds (and the discomfort of drawing leaning up against a wall while it is drizzling!) are not comparable. Place is often very important to a story, and if you can get a feel for it on the ground, you always should. Even if it's not possible to visit a specific location, there is usually a way to find some immersive research opportunities. If I am between projects and feeling stuck, I will usually take a sketchbook to a gallery or museum and just have a wander around. That said, I have never been someone who has been good at sitting in a café or on a train drawing people.*

I think the more you draw the better you get, and I have found that after each book I have done my hand has got more confident and my drawings better. I hope this trajectory continues. I've changed my material preferences, experimented with different mediums and ways of working, but ultimately drawing is the most important thing, and if I haven't drawn enough I can see it in my output. I do keep a sketchbook, but it is not necessarily just for drawings. I use it for writing, thumbnailing and ideas. I tend to mostly draw for a specific purpose, project or idea. I enjoy doing life drawing and sketching in museums, which is one of the few times I draw with no objective.

I think my 'way of drawing' has perhaps emerged specifically to serve graphic storytelling. With these long-form books, in order to be able to tell a story over 200 pages, I have definitely developed a style that enables me to work fast and consistently.

Why did I undertake an MA in Animation? Honestly, I was having a bit of a career crisis! Being an illustrator, for me anyway, is a juggling act. I have the projects I love – graphic novels – and the projects I enjoy but maybe aren't my passion, and then things purely for making money and surviving. I did the MA as a moment to pause and learn new skills and work out where I wanted to go next. But I am also a university lecturer, and pragmatically I knew that having an MA makes working in this world easier. After I finished I realized that I wasn't an animator, but an illustrator who liked making my drawings move. This was a useful realization, and the skills I took away from the MA have been invaluable. Not least, I discovered how much I loved to work in charcoal.

Charcoal and soft pencils (palomino blackwings) are my current materials of choice. But I also still love to work in brush and ink and reed pen. I definitely favour line-based working. I've tried to work with shape but it's not the way my brain works. I like materials that allow for unexpected line variations. I hate fineliners and anything that has a predictable and static line. I like materials that leave traces; splashes, dusting, smudges and textures. I add my colour after, always digitally. I like the colour to be flat and matt and to let the texture and detail of the hand-drawn line work take the lead. Colour is something I have struggled with, and I am still learning and improving.

Drawing and Applied Illustration

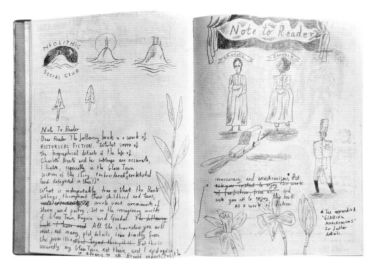

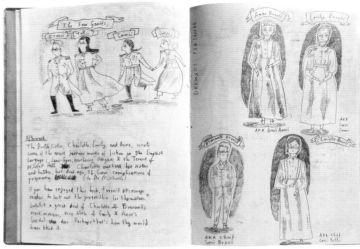

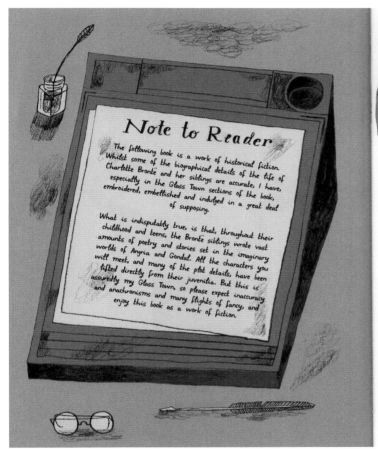

Top: Sketchbook developmental work for Isabel Greenberg's
Glass Town (Jonathan Cape, 2020).
Above and following spread: Interior pages from *Glass Town*.

Isabel Greenberg

Drawing and Applied Illustration

Isabel Greenberg

Jon McNaught
Quiet visual drama

Alongside his acclaimed cover designs for *The London Review of Books* and regular work in editorial illustration for publications including *The New York Times*, *The Wall Street Journal* and *The New Yorker*, London-based Jon McNaught is perhaps best known for his distinctive and distinguished authorship of highly atmospheric graphic novels such as *Birchfield Close* (2010), *Dockwood* (2012) and *Kingdom* (2018) with the publisher Nobrow. In all of these books, McNaught imbues everyday lives with a profound sense of the unsaid. His artworks are predominantly 'shape-led' rather than linear, perhaps influenced by his work as a printmaker. Drawing therefore informs and supports his work in less direct but nonetheless equally important ways, as he explains:

Drawing was always my favourite pastime as a kid. I probably spent most evenings carefully copying characters from books in coloured pencils or felt-tipped pens or whatever I could get my hands on. It was the one thing that I could concentrate on and get lost in. It didn't matter whether I was copying Asterix panels, illustrations from Erik the Viking, or drawing the cast of Sonic the Hedgehog, it would make me feel calm and *would make hours fly by. I have very fond memories of late nights under a lamp in my bedroom, trying to learn the magic trick of making a scene come to life on a page. It seems harder now to get lost in the moment of drawing like that, but I think that is what I am still aiming for.*

I had some great art teachers over the years who encouraged my drawing, and at university I learnt a lot from the print technicians (who later became my colleagues). The print rooms are a beautiful place to learn, through curiosity and experimentation. Using different print processes forces you to keep re-learning how to draw and constantly shifts you out of your comfort zone.

I don't draw from direct observation as much as I should. I go through phases, and am always more contented and inspired when I am filling up a sketchbook, but I can't say that I am good at keeping it up all the time. When working on a project, I often take research trips to sketch and take notes, (with Kingdom, for example, I went to museums, campsites and motorway service stations). This is essential to the work, as I need to inhabit the locations to notice the details that bring the drawings to life. As much as *I like drawing from life, often for practicality I take photographs and then sketch at home using the photographs as reference. This way I can zoom into photographs and continue to explore the locations, finding corners that I missed. Some of my favourite images come from snapshots taken from the windows of trains, where you are drifting along past odd scraps of land and the backs of houses. Sometimes even a few sentences scribbled into a notebook can be enough; that way I can describe a scene to myself and reconstruct it later on the page.*

These days when I do draw from life, I try to work at getting the essence of something, rather than an accurate detailed representation. If I look too closely and add all the details I can be lost for an hour drawing the branches of a tree, but still not quite capture it. What I'm interested in now is a sort of 'observational cartooning' – capturing a sense of something in as few marks as possible.

Creating atmosphere and light through shape – I always start with a pencil sketch to create the compositions, and then I work out colours and tones from there. Sometimes I do this by making a small ink thumbnail,

Above: In this early page from *Kingdom*, Jon McNaught sets the scene, the intricately rendered banality of a motorway service station. The family whose trip is at the centre of the book's journey are silently observed from above.
Following spread: McNaught makes very rough initial pencil drawings as he begins to map out the page-by-page 'scenography' of his visual storytelling.

Jon McNaught

or sometimes I make a digital mock-up in Photoshop, but I always spend a lot more time planning the image than actually painting the final piece. When I get to the final artwork, I know exactly what will go where, so I can concentrate on the quality of the individual brush marks. I try to be fairly loose, using the shape of the brush to make shapes, rather than labouring too much over each detail. I am always aiming to be looser and more energetic with my art, but I think I am unfortunately more inclined towards neatness. Lately I've been drawing in my sketchbook with watercolour and ink, without sketching out the lines first. I'm finding this quite liberating, although I have a long way to go before I can get very good results.

Working in the way that I do with shape has taken years of gradual progression. Working as an illustrator has helped push me to attempt to capture more and more varied subjects with my drawings. As a student I worked almost exclusively with black and blue and made very simple scenes, never drawing people or too much detail. Over the years I have gradually learned how to add more colour to my process, as well as more detail. I always avoided drawing people, in particular faces, until it became a necessity for the comics that I wanted to draw. I still have lots of subjects and scenes that I haven't figured out how to capture, so it is an ongoing exploration.

For me, drawing is mainly about the act of paying attention, paying tribute to a subject by spending time with it and carefully recording it on the page. Craft is also important to me, and although I think any medium of drawing is legitimate, a sensitivity to the process and materials is a big part of drawing.

Drawing and Applied Illustration

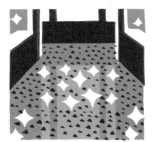

Jon McNaught

Advertising and display

'While advertising design today may appear to be a world of all-singing, all-dancing multimedia, there is still considerable demand for drawing-based illustration'

Until the last decades of the nineteenth century, advertising art had mainly appeared in the form of black and white engraved artworks that were predominantly published as straightforward representations of artefacts or products for sale. The opening up of photographic colour separation in early twentieth-century printing led to rapid recognition of the potential for the artist's image in advertising. In Britain, William Nicholson and his brother-in-law James Pryde had led the way in poster design for advertising under their collective partnership, Beggarstaffs. Company directors began to set up art departments, and the urban landscape was soon transformed by hoardings plastered with large-scale posters scrambling for attention. Magazines, too, were awash with vibrant advertising illustration, as leading artists seized the opportunities that this new era offered. The distinctive work of masters of advertising art such as J. C. Leyendecker in the US, Jules Chéret and Cassandre (Adolphe Jean-Marie Mouron) in France and Frank Newbould in Britain reached huge audiences.

The role of the art director, even before the term became commonplace, was becoming increasingly important. Two of the most influential, visionary figures in British advertising from the 1930s were Frank Pick, chief executive of London Passenger Transport Board, and Jack Beddington, publicity director at Shell. They were responsible for raising standards by persuading some of the finest artists of the day, including Paul Nash, Graham Sutherland and Ben Nicholson, to contribute to their publicity campaigns, as well as those who were more familiar with straddling the fine and applied arts, such as Edward Bawden and Barnett Freedman.

While advertising design today may appear to be a world of all-singing, all-dancing multimedia, there is still considerable demand for drawing-based illustration.

OPPOSITE: An 1891 poster for Cosmydor soap by the great French poster artist Jules Chéret, who was highly regarded for his innovative exploitation of the lithographic process.

Kerry Lemon
Sketchbook to hoarding

The challenges involved in drawing for illustration destined to be experienced at huge scale are, unsurprisingly, markedly different from those faced when creating imagery destined for the intimacy of the printed page. Kerry Lemon has forged a career as a go-to artist for creating projects on large-scale hoardings, prestigious storefronts, light projections in public spaces and much more. Here, she discusses her methods and her passion for drawing.

Drawing is fundamental to the way I view the world. It is my obsession: endlessly fascinating, DEEPLY frustrating, always surprising and, at its best moments, completely fulfilling and meditative. I have always adored the power of drawing; the fact that I can conjure entire worlds to my precise design (both real and imagined) just using a surface and marks. I began with editorial illustration and quickly moved to installation work – large-scale temporary works for luxury brands. Today I no longer 'illustrate' as such, but create large-scale works for the public realm in diverse materials. Drawing remains central to my practice. Everything I make is initially drawn by hand, sketched and then refined again and again, until I create the final artwork ready to be fabricated in wood, glass, metal or stone. Throughout the design process, drawing is also how I communicate with my fabricators – scribbled ideas in meetings, exploring how we can build and assemble the final pieces. I cannot imagine my life without drawing. I love how my line has improved and developed over the years – a clear result of hours spent immersed in the process rewarded by better drawings. It is my very favourite thing to do. A lifelong companion with which to explore and document my desires and adventures.

Working at scale has required a new set of skills. These pieces will be viewed from a variety of angles, heights and distances and also speed – walking, cycling, driving.... A slight wiggle in a line on an A4 sheet of paper will be vast once recreated as part of a hundred-metre artwork. Each project teaches me something new: a new context, landscape, material. I relish the challenge of these projects – the bigger the better. To create such monumental work requires a team of experts. I design and draw everything by hand, then pass these pieces to my artworker, Josh, who is a wizard at converting them to the correct dimensions and file types for the fabrication process. I collaborate with fabricators all over the world – experts in their chosen materials who are able to utilize both traditional and new technologies to create the final artworks.

I'm evangelistic about drawing. Always on a mission to get people to draw. The tragedy of art education is the quick determination of who is 'good' at drawing and who is not. An obsession with product, rather than the process of creation. Finding joy in the process, the sound and texture of dragging pen, brush or pencil across a page will mean you will continue to do it and, as in all things, the more you actually draw, the more you WILL automatically improve – your finished drawings will become better and better. There are no shortcuts. No expensive pens or expert tuition will get you there. Just draw. Draw constantly. Draw everything, all the time. Drawing is all about looking and a regular drawing practice will alter your view of the world. You will begin to see things that you previously ignored. Sitting on the train, you will be acutely aware of the pattern of the seat, the light on the metal railing, the profile of the commuter opposite, the weave of their scarf. Drawing is magic, and I am bewitched by it.

Top: Kerry Lemon at work on the windows of Harvey Nichols department store in London.
Above: A view of one of the final window designs.

Kerry Lemon

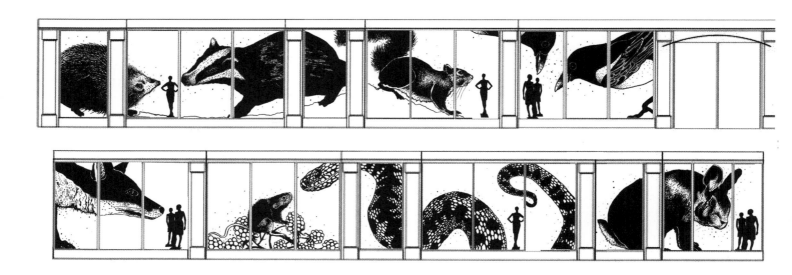

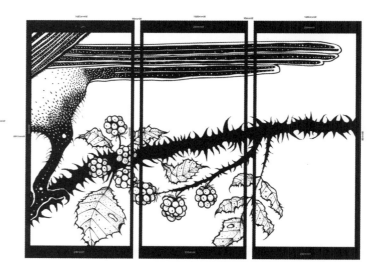

Top: An early draft plan on paper for the window by Kerry Lemon.
Above: A section of the design showing scaling-up measurements.
Opposite: An original ink drawing on paper of a section of the
window, shown above the digitally cleaned-up version.

Drawing and Applied Illustration

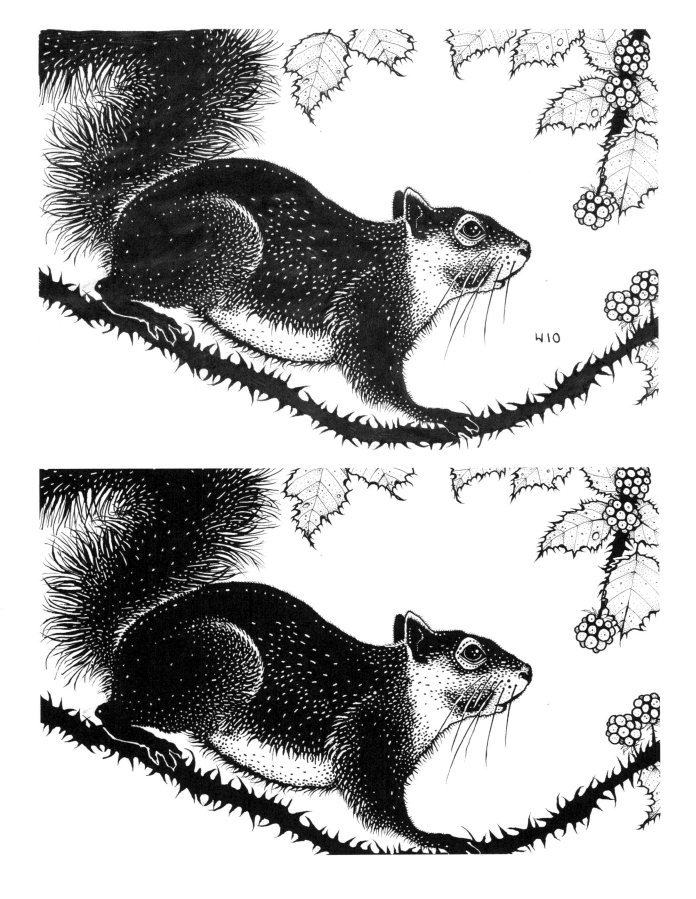

Kerry Lemon

'I proceed to make from memory several very rough diagrams
in pencil of compositions suggested by the different aspects of
the town which I have seen in my rambles'

Frank Newbould
Eliminating detail

During the interwar years, Frank Newbould's distinctive posters were ubiquitous in British cities. For much of his career, the poster was the primary means of reaching a large audience. Often printed in multiple sheets and pasted up in numbered order to make the full image, they were designed to be seen from a distance with maximum visual impact.

Newbould's particular skill was in simplifying complex scenes into flat shapes and colours and organizing them into dynamic, instantly readable compositions. He detailed his working methods in Lesson 23, *Poster Drawing*, one of twenty-five instructional booklets published by The British and Dominions School of Drawing series in the 1920s. Taking as a case study his 1922 poster for the Royal Hotel, Ventnor, he gives an insight into the relationship between observational information-gathering and the process of balancing reality with compositional design needs:

A plan that I often adopt myself, especially when handling landscape posters, is to eliminate as much as possible, especially in the foreground, and to allow myself to elaborate a little more at the point in the composition to which I am attempting to lead the eye. As an example, take my poster of Ventnor. In this, everything else has been reduced to its simplest form so that the utmost value might be got out of the little town nestling against the distant headlands. In this case the eye makes a following movement and the only

feature which really arrests it is the panel of lettering which tells the story and is of course the only reason for the existence of the poster.

Returning to this Ventnor example, I make it a working rule in the case of a commission like this to wander about the place in question for an hour or two and try to get hold of the atmosphere of the place. At the end of that time I shall have decided what the character of the resort is; it may be a place of fashion or it may be of the quaint, old-world type. Also, I shall have noticed that there are two or three points of vantage in or about the town from which a good composition could possibly be made. I then visit these various points, making no sketches, and return to the town, where I proceed to make from memory several very rough diagrams in pencil of compositions suggested by the different aspects of the town which I have seen in my rambles. Very rough scrawls are these, say about two inches by three inches. The most promising of them I then try to elaborate on a slightly larger scale as far as possible from memory. The reason why I do not do this part of the work on the spot is that when the landscape is not actually before my eyes my sense of composition has freer play; and as I fill in the various landmarks from memory the tendency is for them to appear in the place that I think best from the point of view of composition, which may be a little at variance with the actual positions.

However it is much more important, at any rate from the poster artist's point of view, that the composition should be perfectly right than that it should be exactly topographically accurate. The various features in the landscape should be regarded as isolated notes of music which it is the task of the poster artist to arrange into one striking and harmonious chord. One cannot of course take too many liberties with a place or it ceases to be that place. The atmosphere is the great thing to try to catch.

The next step is to take my memory sketch back to the spot from which I obtained the impression on which it was based, and compare it with the actual scene. Probably I find that I have placed, say, the pier in an impossible position and it must be altered more in accordance with the facts. And so I go on, in the end effecting a compromise between what I think ought to be and what is. I then take written notes of the most important colour features, but I rarely make any outside colour sketches, preferring to rely on my memory and written notes. I have done a very considerable amount of outdoor colour work in the past, and it is probably on that account that I do not now find it necessary. Nevertheless, I cannot too strongly urge the beginner to go direct to Nature in the first place, otherwise there is bound to be a subconscious tendency to borrow colour schemes and compositions from the work of other men.

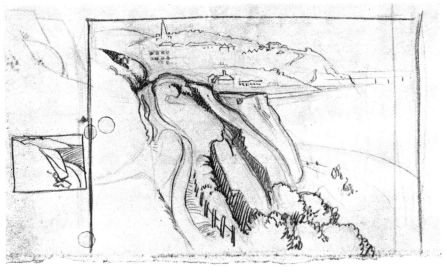

Top: Frank Newbould's method of researching his travel posters involved getting to know his subject by making a thorough tour of the site and then making very quick sketches of the key features, as in these drawings of Ventnor, Isle of Wight. Above: The final poster for the Royal Hotel, Ventnor, rendered in Newbould's signature simplified flat colour.

Frank Newbould

Humour

'Graphic satire and caricature
have long been seen as among the
most effective ways of puncturing
pomposity in all its forms'

Visual humour has probably been with us since humankind first made representational marks on a surface. There are certainly plenty of examples to be found in surviving artworks and decorated artefacts from the ancient Greek and Roman civilizations. Poking fun at human failings and eccentricities was much favoured in wood carvings and decorative embellishments throughout the Middle Ages. Around 1500, Albrecht Dürer and Leonardo da Vinci both indulged in what has since become known as caricature – the distortion and exaggeration of an individual's features for comic effect – and the eighteenth century saw William Hogarth's pictorial satire and social comment powerfully influence the genre. Graphic satire and caricature have long been seen as some of the most effective ways of puncturing pomposity in all its forms, particularly in the political arena, and the drawn image is highly valued for its role in describing and reflecting upon the absurdity of everyday life. Humorous drawing can be found across most areas of illustration, whether as an accompaniment to comedic writing or in authorial visual work. Throughout the nineteenth and early twentieth centuries, the 'visual gag' was generally delivered in the form of elaborate, even epic scenes, often heavily populated and executed with great skill by highly trained draughtsmen. While we may still admire the skills of such artists, the humour often seems laborious to a modern audience, and the one-off newspaper or magazine 'cartoon' is now generally associated with a manner of drawing that is executed in a 'light' or non-realistic manner.

OPPOSITE: E. H. Shepard is best known for his illustrations for A. A. Milne's *Winnie the Pooh,* but he was also one of the most prolific humorous artists of his day, contributing to many periodicals including this 1935 edition of the legendary *Punch* magazine.

Drawing and Applied Illustration

'It's mostly just through pen or pencil on paper, seeing where it goes.
If it makes me smile it might be going somewhere'

Paul Slater
Master of the absurd

Paul Slater stands out in the world of contemporary illustration and painting for his anachronistic fusion of formal, classical drawing and painting skills with a highly personal sense of the absurd. His world is populated by earnest military types, genial cowboys, cowgirls and other comic-book heroes. For his illustration commissions, he has tended to work primarily with acrylic paints. It is the incongruity of such virtuoso formal skills being employed to realize a particularly British sense of nonsense that makes Slater's world so unique and compelling. For many years his work has graced leading international magazines and newspapers, illustrating journalistic writing with surreal visual comedy. He now devotes his time primarily to painting.

Perhaps surprisingly, Slater is firmly with Ardizzone when analysing his relationship with drawing and the evolution of his methods. He points to two particular moments of epiphany. The first of these was the excellent life-drawing teaching he recalls receiving as an Art Foundation student at Burnley art school in the 1970s, although he feels that overall at art school, the greatest value came from learning from fellow students. After going on to study Illustration at Maidstone College of Art, it was during his subsequent MA studies at the Royal College of Art that a second key event was to influence the direction of his work:

At the RCA I did draw people from life in the sketchbook all the time, but one day I was on a London bus, going around Hyde Park or somewhere, people-watching from the top deck, and I saw this particular guy, he was bent double with a huge backpack. And he was wearing menacingly tight blue shorts, with a baseball cap over long hair. Totally absurd. I went to draw him but it was too late, he'd gone. When I got into college I drew him from memory. I realized then that I could do this and that I could do it in a consistent way.

It's a process I suppose. I got quite good at taking a drawing from my head and transferring it to paper through drawing. I'm trying now to do that with oil paint. In a way it's more drawing-based. I think I was a bit sloppy before. I'm trying to get more spontaneity onto the canvas, more movement and gestures, less defined, softer.

Paradoxically, he feels that in order to allow for more expression in the painting, the planning through drawing needs to be more meticulous: 'Everything flows from drawing. I like to plan methodically.' But the initial visual ideas are arrived at through a much more intuitive kind of drawing in the sketchbook:

I just start drawing. It might be a cowboy or a king. I might get two or three decent ideas. It's mostly just through pen or pencil on paper, seeing where it goes. If it makes

me smile it might be going somewhere. It's not intellectual. I gave a talk at an art school conference about 'the absurd' a while ago. I felt a bit like a sore thumb. Everyone seemed to have carefully planned their absurdity. I don't work like that. I just think stupid things through drawing.

When a drawing asserts itself as a subject for a final painting, it is squared up mechanically to be transferred to canvas. Of course, this kind of drawing for illustration is much more controlled and practical. Lynton Lamb devotes a chapter to this process in his book *Preparation for Painting* (Penguin, 1960). Ensuring that the final painting or illustration is marked up to exactly the same proportions (by multiplying the width and then the length by the same percentage, rather than adding the same measurement to each, as I have seen happen so often!), a pencil grid is laid over the original drawing, divided into equal squares. These can then be enlarged by the same proportions onto the final surface for painting, allowing the original drawing to follow the exact same composition by checking square by square, just as was practised by Italian Renaissance painters. In Slater's case, the scaled-up sketch is initially painted roughly with thin washes of colour, through which the pencil work is still visible, ready for over-painting.

Above and following spread: Examples of Paul Slater's illustrations for *The Times* newspaper's 'Eating Out' pages, showing the rough colour sketches with scaling-up grids.

Paul Slater

Drawing and Applied Illustration

Paul Slater

Reportage and graphic commentary

'Visual journalism is, and always has been, a means by which the artist can comment subjectively – poetically, satirically, subversively – on the chosen subject'

It is probably fair to say that this particular branch of illustration is the most deeply rooted in observational drawing of them all. In his seminal book on the subject, *The Artist as Reporter,* Paul Hogarth lamented what he believed was the inferior status traditionally accorded to the documentary artist, observing that 'Journalism, like detective fiction, weighs lightly on the scales of art criticism'.

Artists have engaged in 'reporting' visually on events since the earliest recorded history. For much of this time, visual journalism was used as propaganda to present versions of war, heroic deeds or pageantry in a manner that suited the requirements of its sponsor. But it was often also the only way that the general public could catch a glimpse, albeit a selective one, of far-off worlds and events that we are now accustomed to being bombarded with through our ubiquitous screens. The pages of newspapers and magazines through much of the nineteenth and twentieth centuries were filled with engravings and later direct reproductions of drawings made by artists whose works were often at least partially made from direct observation on location. Hogarth himself was one of the most celebrated of artist-reporters, travelling the world to observe and record through pencil drawing.

Visual journalism is, and always has been, a means by which the artist can comment subjectively – poetically, satirically, subversively – on the chosen subject. With photography in courtrooms having been banned on and off in many cultures, 'artists' impressions' are still used for trial reporting. In some places, including the United Kingdom, direct drawing at a trial is now banned, so the sketches are produced of necessity from a mixture of immediate memory and available photographic reference, with generally mixed results. In 1961 Ronald Searle spent a year in Jerusalem making drawings at the trial of the Nazi war criminal Adolf Eichmann for *Life* magazine. While in Israel he also tracked down and visited survivors of the Holocaust, including the man who led the escape through the sewers of Warsaw and another who tried to negotiate the exchange of trucks for Jews in concentration camps. Writing about it in the Association of Illustrators Newsletter in January 1977, he recalled: *'I drew them and many others… until my portfolio was complete enough to give the trial the aspect of horror that lay behind that cold recounting in the court.'*

OPPOSITE: Laura Carlin is one of the most admired illustrators of the twenty-first century. Her professional work in picturebooks and other areas of the arts is built on a strong background in reportage drawing. This detail from one of her full-page images comes from her time spent observing daily life in Japan while studying at the Royal College of Art in 2004, and was reproduced in her limited-edition book *Ten Days in Tokyo* (RCA).

Searle was an experienced reportage artist, having travelled widely, including to Poland and Yugoslavia with Paul Hogarth in 1947 to make drawings that highlighted the plight of war refugees, and later across America to make documentary drawings for both *Life* and *Holiday* magazines. It was his harrowing drawings, made in unimaginable conditions while imprisoned by the Japanese for most of the Second World War, that gave him an involuntary initial grounding. Summing up his thoughts on reportage illustration as a whole in the same article he wrote:

Physically the work is tough and mentally it is anguishing. It is only possible to do reportage work if one has a solid grounding in drawing. Reportage has to have flesh, bones, and above all, life in it. One is not illustrating, but pushing one's nose into life. On top of that, one must have something to say – however crass. Reportage is not reporting, it is opinion and comment that takes it away from journalism into (minor) art.

ABOVE AND OPPOSITE: Ronald Searle documented his incarceration in a Japanese prisoner of war camp in hundreds of drawings on scavenged scraps of paper. They span from the prisoners' early months on a troop ship to the unimaginable horrors that were to await them upon arrival in Singapore. A selection of the drawings was published in the book *Forty Drawings* (Cambridge University Press, 1946) on Searle's eventual return to his hometown of Cambridge.

Ronald Searle.
Bukit-Timah Singapore 1942

David Hughes
Covid diary

David Hughes's work as an illustrator and graphic author over the last forty years has been profoundly influential. As well as working regularly for newspapers and magazines in the UK and US, he has authored numerous graphic novels and picturebooks and created designs for opera in Italy. His work is deeply rooted in the drawn line as an uncompromising and primary means of expression. Here, he writes about a project undertaken during the COVID-19 lockdowns in the UK, and about drawing in general, in a typically freewheeling 'stream of consciousness' manner.

On waking this morning at about 4:45 a.m. – which is the usual time these days, within thirty minutes or so with a cup of tea in bed I reach for the sketchbook on the side table. Outside the rainfall is biblical. It has been almost a daily routine like this since early March, drawing in bed, sketching in secret, before the day realizes. It helps me feel I might have achieved something for the remainder of the day (sometimes) – like that smug sensation of getting up, getting dressed to go for a run before work, before the masses stir. Something I haven't done for a century.... There's a selection of pencil stubs of various grades, from the humble HB up to an exotic 9B fighting for space on the bedside table-top. A pencil sharpener and an old ashtray to catch any pencil shavings. Most mornings I don't have an idea what I'm going to attempt

to put on paper, this morning my brain is a lump of flintstone. Pencil has always been my weapon of choice. This morning before the sketching I completed a simple Guardian Codeword, also in pencil, I like the satisfying act of lettering the squares. But now I'm looking at a blank page. I've switched on BBC Radio 4 for the news, the headlines, hoping something might trigger something. Other mornings my sleeping brain may have already concocted some ideas before I've woken, but not this morning. The thunderstorms dominate the items. It is Instagram that has been the destiny of these daily drawings, that and the outside possibility that there could be a book out of this, not a chance, it would take a year to come to publication even if a publisher was interested....anyway to date it's Instagram I'm polluting, clogging up the feed, busking for hearts, farming for encouragement from front-line artists and other apostles who trail me. But recently I've been finding it difficult to produce any worthwhile sketching...I'm tired of this virus, I'm sick and bored with the daily Downing Street so-called briefings, I want to stop but it's as the government repeats, 'tiny steps' to get back to normal. I have, as a bookmark on this bedside table-top, an auction-house bidding card in a lovely black Franklin Gothic Condensed style typeface – the auctioneer's hymn, 'going, going, gone!' worms into my mind, this would make a good title of

a drawing for perhaps a final Instagram post, something else I want to get off.

'What Day is It?' has also been a recurring theme for my drawings. I write it out – I've turned on YouTube, there's a Bob Dylan live recording from back in the 1960s. I end up doing a head, filling the page face-on, it's experimental. I'm pushing the medium of graphite as far as a bed-ridden doodle will allow me. I'm almost excited at the potential of what I'm trying out, a new technique that is so simple, why haven't I done it before? It is a fleeting satisfying moment, a quick fix. Within half an hour it's on Instagram.

I love drawing with a pencil. I've always liked the humble pencil. In the 1980s up until around 1989 a good proportion of my commissioned illustration output was predominately pencil, charcoal and collage. If I did use a pen, most of it was faking spontaneity, repeating an image on another sheet over the original 'sketch', ironing out the imperfections with the aid of a lightbox. Tedious. Soul-destroying. A combination of events encouraged me to switch almost entirely to a dip-pen and ink. The reproduction quality of any subtlety in a pencil drawing would disappear, especially in a newspaper, coupled with the fact my originals were the size of a dining room table-top seating up to ten diners.

My intelligence is expressed through drawing, my ideas evolve more freely through the physical act of drawing, more often

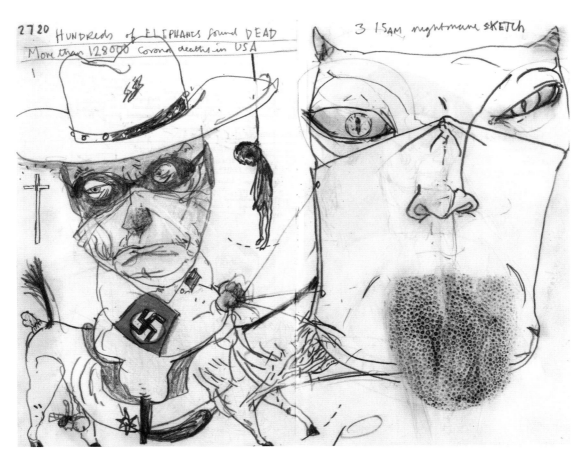

Above and following spread: In his freewheeling, 'stream of consciousness' 2020 Covid diary, David Hughes fused personal experience with television news bulletins, political commentary and satire.

David Hughes

than not it is a mystery. It is a gift some say, I frequently answer it is a curse. But thank God I do draw.

From as early as I can remember I was always drawing. Maybe being brought up as an 'only child' (although I had three brothers and a sister, by the time I was eighteen months old they had all left home), it was an escape, a way to entertain myself. I would draw imaginary cowboys, footballers, pop groups, give them names, draw their portraits. Never wrote stories, just invented characters.

At eight my nativity drawing was declared the best in the class by the class bully, John Woods, mine being the only solo effort. All the others had been group creations. At sixteen, at secondary school, for one afternoon a handful of us had the opportunity to draw from life, two student teachers

who posed for us (fully clothed). I couldn't believe I was at school and actually drawing from a model. Very important afternoon. It was the first time I'd ever drawn a living person from life. Life drawing became my way of getting through art school (Twickenham College of Technology) from sixteen years of age to leaving at twenty and attempting to go freelance. For two, maybe three years of that course I also used a sketchbook, but the practice slowly dwindled out. During the freelance career a sketchbook became a luxury – something I might take away but rarely use (does a plumber take on holiday his bag of plungers and blow lamps?). Maybe I might use a sketchbook for trying out story ideas, but that was all.

It was Walking The Dog (Jonathan Cape, 2009) that brought me back to using

a sketchbook, and I've used one ever since. Drawing events from your own past is a powerful method of evoking memories that have almost disappeared. In Walking The Dog I surprised myself with likenesses from forty years or so ago through drawing without the aid of photographs....

Of course, drawing with ink raises the bar – it focuses the mind, the indelible mark on that expensive sheet of white paper coupled with the process of leaving it until the deadline is almost flying past was the way I worked as a professional illustrator. These days it's mostly pencil. The drawings here are all drawn this past thirteen months (2020–21), and most are created in bed and therefore in graphite. The briefing drawings are all done live, as are the newsreaders.

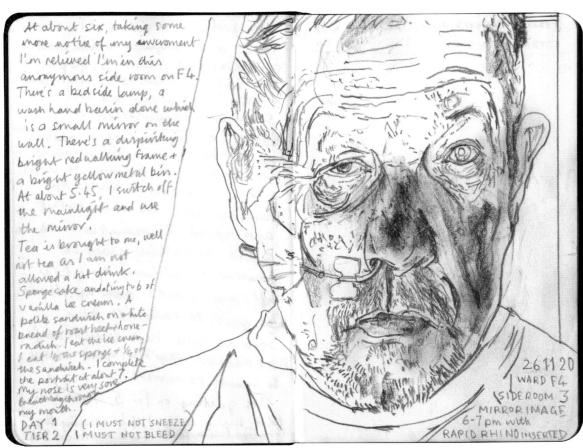

At about six, taking some
more notice of my environment
I'm relieved I'm in this
anonymous side room on F4.
There's a bedside lamp, a
wash hand basin above which
is a small mirror on the
wall. There's a dispiriting
bright red walking frame +
a bright yellow metal bin.
At about 5.45, I switch off
the mainlight and use
the mirror.
Tea is brought to me, well
not tea as I am not
allowed a hot drink.
Sponge cake and a tiny tub of
vanilla ice cream. A
polite sandwich on white
bread of roast beef + horse-
radish. I eat the ice cream,
I eat ½ the sponge + ¼ of
the sandwich. I complete
the portrait at about 7.
My nose is very sore
breathing through
my mouth.

DAY 1 (I MUST NOT SNEEZE)
TIER 2 I MUST NOT BLEED

26 11 20
WARD F4
SIDE ROOM 3
MIRROR IMAGE
6-7 pm with
RAPID RHINO INSERTED

TAKING JENNY'S POINT
BJ
AND WASH YOUR HANDS
22nd March 2020

SAVE LIVES

JENNY HARRIES

MOMENT OF NATIONAL EMERGENCY

Monday 23 March 2020   1 FORM of Exercise A day

David Hughes

'I did it with my own little pencil, nary a camera. Just drawing.
I felt I could do better, be clearer and more precise'

Robert Weaver:
The bare essentials

Described by the author Alexander Roob as 'the most significant American illustrator of his time', Robert Weaver, or 'The Weave' as he was often affectionately known by his students at the School of Visual Arts (SVA) in New York City, has only recently begun to receive the acclaim and wider appreciation that he deserves. Weaver's importance to the field of documentary drawing or 'visual journalism' is immeasurable. His impact exerts itself not only through his innovative illustration works for major US magazines and journals of the 1950s to 1970s, but also through his work alongside Marshall Arisman in building and teaching on the renowned MFA Illustration as Visual Essay programme at SVA from its inception in 1984.

Roob's observation opens the essay that accompanies one of Weaver's previously unpublished experimental picturebooks, *A Pedestrian View: The Vogelman Diary*, brought out by Verlag Kettler in 2012. Produced at a time when his eyesight was failing, *The Vogelman Diary* takes the form of a sequence of painterly gouache images of urban life seen from pavement level, each one with roughly pencilled text in capitals beneath the image. The text reads across the pages, obliquely connecting to the images.

Weaver was uncompromising in regarding his work as highly personal, and was known for his 'take it or leave it' attitude to many of those who commissioned his work. He had never studied Illustration or Commercial Art, but spent two years in Venice studying Classical Painting at the Academia while staying with an aunt. In a wide-ranging interview with Wendy Coates-Smith in a 1981 issue of *Illustrators*, he recalled how he fell in love with New York City, to which he had moved on his return from Italy, and where he would spend whole days drawing:

It was such a visual city – it still is. I used to ride on the elevated subway, getting off at various platforms and making drawings. I went everywhere. I would get on the subway in the morning with a sketchbook, and didn't care where, and would end up somewhere in Queens or Brooklyn. I would get off at some arbitrary station and would start walking in this alien land making sketches. By the end of the day I would come back with twenty drawings, rather like a hunter coming back with some fish or some rabbits.

Weaver claimed to have little knowledge of art beyond the Renaissance at the time.

He had hoped to become a mural painter. But his gritty, direct approach to drawing brought him commissions in the early 1950s to create visual reports for magazine features on crime. In characteristically prickly manner, he recalled:

I think my drawing style seemed to be so crude alongside the styles of the established commercial illustrators of the time... my way of drawing human beings seemed to art directors to be a way appropriate to the drawing of criminals. To the advertising man, I obviously represented the outsider, somebody who didn't consume the proper products, who hadn't been to the right finishing schools. Clearly I would be the right person to draw a criminal.

But Weaver's reputation grew, his visual reportage challenging the ubiquitous use (and perceived higher status) of journalistic photography. His visual essays were commissioned by, among others, *Esquire*, *Life*, *Sports Illustrated* and *Fortune*. At the latter he was commissioned in the late 1950s by Leo Leonni, who later became a renowned children's picturebook-maker:

Leonni was sending me out to do coverage of foundries and industries. He was

224   Drawing and Applied Illustration

Above and following spread: Robert Weaver managed to fuse observational drawing
with illustration to create gritty, direct reportage of highly charged moments.
p. 226, below: In *A Pedestrian View: The Vogelman Diaries*, Weaver enigmatically
juxtaposes painting and crudely written text.

Robert Weaver

a superb art director and helped me at a time when I didn't know what the hell I was doing. He taught me a couple of lessons... I went out with a sketchpad and pencil. I did a lot of drawings and then I coloured them up later. I did it with my own little pencil, nary a camera. Just drawing. I felt I could do better, be clearer and more precise.

As a teacher at SVA, Weaver was legendary, greatly admired by generations of students for his honesty and integrity. One of his former students, Kevin McCloskey, later recalled that when he and his fellow students gathered for a group critique on a project to draw construction activity, Weaver was less than impressed by the volume of work produced:

He told us he found our excuses much more fascinating than our drawings, and said he hoped we could someday get that sort of narrative power in our artwork. Brutal. He insisted that we draw from life rather than photos whenever possible. He was very keen on what historians call primary material. He told a story about an art student he met at a bus stop. The student was headed up to the picture file at the New York Public Library.

'What sort of photo reference are you looking for?' Weaver asked.

'A bus.' said the student.

'What sort of bus?' he asked.

'A regular bus. A New York City bus.'

'Why don't you stay on this corner and draw a bus stopped in traffic?'

'Photos are better', said the student as he hopped on the bus.

Drawing and Applied Illustration

chemical
worker

John Minton
Reportage for advertising

During the late 1940s and into the mid-1950s, John Minton was one of the most celebrated painter–illustrators of his generation. He was evangelical in his belief in the role of observation as the key to visual art as a whole. His passion for drawing and for the importance of a love of *subject,* meant that he became increasingly alienated from the world of fine art as the post-war mood of neoromantic landscape was swept away by the arrival of Abstract Expressionism in Britain. But alongside his paintings, the best of his prolific output of illustration work has, over time, become at least as highly appreciated for the passion that he put into it.

In a 1952 lecture given to students of the City of Birmingham College of Arts & Crafts titled *Speculations on the Contemporary Painter*, Minton spoke about the importance of a deep engagement with subject if the artist is to develop and grow. After observing the tendency of many art students to throw together a few bits and pieces in order to draw or paint a still life in the hope that 'something will happen', he asserts:

It will only happen if it is really done with love, otherwise it won't.... It's like a blacksmith having all the appropriate tools, but no fire. He can hammer away indefinitely but nothing will happen – not even abstract sculpture. For it's something to do with having a real love for the subject, having a real anxiety it will escape: not just tolerating it as a possible subject, but loving it. Drawing is the key, the preliminary enquiry, and is so closely bound up with the art of painting that the two cannot be separated.

These strongly held sentiments are made visual as much in his illustration work as in his paintings. In one of his most celebrated books, the travel journal *Time Was Away*, his eighty-seven line drawings and eight four-colour letterpress line-block prints are the result of three weeks of travelling around Corsica in high summer with the writer Alan Ross, making drawing after drawing from direct observation. Some of these were used in the book as they were, others were worked up and developed into more graphic form with greater use of solid blacks to give more weight to the page. And of course the drawings underpinned the printmaking process through which the eight four-colour plates were executed. It is Minton's absolute

immersion in his subject that makes this book such an evocative classic.

But the kind of 'love of subject' that Minton spoke about in his lecture was not dependent on that subject being as obviously seductive as a Mediterranean island. Shortly after the trip to Corsica, as his reputation continued to grow, Minton was commissioned by the Imperial Smelting Corporation, through the advertising agents Everetts, to make drawings at their Avonmouth plant near Bristol. This was part of Everetts's enlightened policy of commissioning a range of leading artists of the day to document visually the processes employed by their various industrial clients. Minton made a number of drawings in pen and wash on location of these great industrial interiors, populated by workers performing their various tasks, dwarfed by the great metal shapes. Some of these were then formalized into illustrations that were more carefully composed and simplified for reproduction in advertisements. These appeared in trade journals as well as mass-market publications such as *Punch* magazine and *The Times* newspaper.

Above: In the late 1940s, John Minton distilled expansive location drawings
and paintings into carefully composed black and white illustrations,
designed to be reproduced at small scale in various trade publications.

John Minton

Illustration
and photography

'Making the reference material serve the artist's
creative vision, as distinct from allowing it to
lead the way, is of paramount importance'

Robert Weaver's evangelical advocacy for drawing from direct observation can be seen primarily in the context of education, even though Weaver himself pushed it further into the making of illustration for reproduction. While photography can even be damaging when learning to draw, it is and has been throughout its history an important aid to many illustrators, directly and indirectly. How it is used by the artist is crucial. Making the reference material serve the artist's creative vision, as distinct from allowing it to lead the way, is of paramount importance. Highly representational illustration has drifted in out of fashion over the years, but this kind of work, often depicting groups of figures in carefully posed 'tableaux', has inevitably involved working from studio photography of models in the tradition of such masters as Norman Rockwell in America and Harry Hants in Britain. The most successful of such artists would command high fees for magazine covers, allowing them to pay models and run their own photography studios. Most of the artists working in this idiom in the mid-twentieth century would have had a solid grounding in formal painting from observation before working primarily from photographic reference, giving them the knowledge and means through which to understand the underlying three-dimensional forms behind the two-dimensional photographs.

The subtler and perhaps deeper influence of photography is revealed when speaking with many illustrators who cite the work of particular photographers as major influences on their approach to their work. We have seen how important the work of photographers, notably that of Josef Koudelka, has been to Bill Bragg's approach to image-making. Similarly, the Canadian illustrator and picturebook-maker Sydney Smith has spoken of the profound influence of street photographers such as Lee Friedlander and Robert Frank on his work and Jon McNaught has explained how his own photographs, taken on location at museums, campsites, motorway service stations and from windows of trains, play an important role in building up a library of visually anecdotal reference for 'sense of place'. What all of these diverse approaches to making use of photography share is a clear understanding of the need for it to be subordinate to the artist's purpose.

OPPOSITE: Normal Rockwell's cover illustrations for the *Saturday Evening Post* were arrived at through a series of detailed preparatory drawings from his carefully staged studio photography.

Postscript:
A word about

Style

Facility [in drawing] *is a dangerous thing. Where there is too much technical ease the brain stops criticising. Don't let the hand fall into a smart way of putting the mind to sleep.*
John Sloan

When embarking on a course in illustration, many students express their urgent desire to acquire a 'style'. Younger students especially yearn for a visual formula that is instantly identifiable as their own, and are often convinced that this is the sole aim of their studies – to be instantly recognizable through their work, like so many of their illustration heroes.

The word 'style' has many meanings, but in this context as a noun it is defined by the Cambridge English Dictionary as:

a way of doing something, especially one that is typical of a person, group of people, place or time.

There is nothing easier than manufacturing a 'style': a particular formula of dots, squiggles or cubes, a very specific colour palette or manner of using a particular medium. A personal horror of mine is the style of fake spontaneity – carefully controlled swishes and swirls, designed to be mistaken for preparatory underdrawing – to give a 'sketchbook aesthetic'. Of course, another of the word's meanings is closely connected to the idea of fashion or trend. Illustration in the 1980s and 1990s was especially style-driven, with many superficially seductive but facile stylistic tricks on display by practitioners whose work has long disappeared from sight. Graduates from illustration courses would regularly enjoy whirlwind stellar exposure for three to four years before being cruelly cast aside by agents and commissioners in favour of 'the next big thing'. This damaged the standing and status of illustration for some time.

Paradoxically, a genuine individual visual vocabulary can only emerge unsought, through the long process of searching instead for a way to make sense of something seen or imagined or both. Through intense focus on the subject itself, rather than the marks being made in response to it, gradually, involuntarily and inevitably an identity forces itself through and imposes itself upon the artist, like it or not. Or, as the information for potential applicants to Marshall Arisman's MFA programme in Illustration as Visual Essay at New York's School of Visual Arts states, 'It begins with developing a personal vision. Vision is not style.'

The End

BIBLIOGRAPHY

Ardizzone, Edward, *The Born Illustrator*, in *Motif No 1* (ed. Ruari McLean), London: The Shenval Press Ltd, 1958

— *Some Random Thoughts on the Art of Illustration*, in *Ark: The Journal of the Royal College of Art*, No. 11, London: RCA, 1954

Bang, Molly, *Picture This: How Pictures Work*, San Francisco: Chronicle, 2000

Brown, Christopher, *An Alphabet of London*, London: Merrell, 2012

Carlin, Laura, *Ten Days in Tokyo*, London: Royal College of Art, 2004

Carline, Richard, *Draw They Must: A History of the Teaching and Examining of Art*, London: Edward Arnold, 1968

Davis, Paul (ed.), *Drawing SVA*, Issue 1, School of Visual Arts: New York, 1997

Garth, Paul, *Creative Pencil Drawing*, London: Studio Vista, 1964

Hayes, Colin, *Grammar of Drawing: for Artists and Designers*, London: Studio Vista, 196

Heller, Steven and Arisman, Marshall, *The Education of the Illustrator*, New York: Allworth Press, 2000

Hobbs, Eric, *Drawing for Advertising*, London: The Studio, 1956

Hogarth, Paul, *Drawing Architecture: A Creative Approach*, New York: Watson-Guptill, 1973

Hogarth, Paul, *The Artist as Reporter*, London: Gordon Fraser, 1986

Hogarth, Paul, *Paul Hogarth's American Album*, London: Lion and Unicorn Press, 1973

Jacobs, Ted Seth, *Drawing with an Open Mind: Reflections from a Drawing Teacher*, New York: Watson-Guptill Publications, 1991

Jones, Barbara, *Water-colour Painting: A Practical Guide*, London: A&C Black, 1960

Kingman, Lee, *The Illustrator's Notebook*, Boston: The Horn Book Inc., 1978

Kingston, Angela, *What is Drawing?*, London: Black Dog Publishing, 2003

Lamb, Lynton, *Drawing for Illustration*, Oxford: Oxford University Press, 1962

Lamb, Lynton, *Preparation for Painting*, Oxford: Oxford University Press, 1954

Lamb, Lynton, *The True Illustrator*, in *Motif No 2*, ed. Ruari McLean), London: The Shenval Press Ltd, 1959

Llewellyn, Sacha and Liss, Paul, *Evelyn Dunbar: The Lost Works*, Chichester: Pallant House Gallery, 2015

Lobel, Michael, *John Sloan: Drawing on Illustration*, New Haven: Yale University Press, 2014

Mackie, George, *Lynton Lamb: Illustrator*, London: The Scolar Press, 1978

Marr, Andrew, *A Short Book About Drawing*, London: Quadrille Publishing Ltd, 2013

Martin, Douglas, *The Telling Line*, London: Julia McRae, 1989

McLanathan, Richard, *The Brandywine Heritage*, New York: Brandywine River Museum/NY Graphic Soc. Ltd, 1971

Micklewright, Keith, *Drawing: Mastering the Language of Visual Expression*, London: Laurence King Publishing, 2005

Minton, John, *Speculations on the Contemporary Painter*, Birmingham: Birmingham College of Arts and Crafts, 1952

Read, Herbert, *Education Through Art*, London: Faber & Faber, 1946

Roob, Alexander, *Inside the Reactor*, in *Robert Weaver, a Pedestrian View: The Vogelman Diary*, Bönen, Dortmund: Verlag Kettler, 2012

Ruskin, John, *The Elements of Drawing: In Three Letters to Beginners*, London: Smith, Elder & Co., 1857

Salisbury, Martin, *The Illustrated Dust Jacket, 1920–1970*, London: Thames & Hudson, 2017

Salisbury, Martin, *The Snail that Climbed the Eiffel Tower and Other Works by John Minton*, Norwich: Mainstone Press, 2017

Schwarcz, Joseph H., *Ways of the Illustrator: Visual Communication in Children's Literature*, Chicago: American Library Association, 1982

Simpson, Ian, *Drawing: Seeing and Observation*, London: A & C Black, 1981

Stanton, Jane, *The Art of Life Drawing*, London: Mitchel Beazley, 1990

Topolski, Feliks, *The London Spectacle, 1935*, London: The Bodley Head, 1935

Various, *The London Art Schools*, London: Tate Publishing, 2016

Vernon Lord, John, *Drawing Upon Drawing: 50 Years of Illustrating*, Brighton: University of Brighton, 2014

White, Gabriel, *Edward Ardizzone: Artist and Illustrator*, London: The Bodley Head, 1979

White, Gwen, *A Book of Pictorial Perspective*, London: John Murray, 1954

CREDITS

2 © Yann Kebbi

4 Collection Martin Salisbury

7 a Charles Edmund Brock: study for 7b. Author's collection

7 b Charles Edmund Brock. From *Holmes Breakfast Table* series by Oliver Wendell Holmes. London: J. M. Dent & Co., 1902

9 Courtesy the Lynton Lamb estate

10, 11 Stanley Badmin, courtesy Chris Beetles Gallery for the S R Badmin Estate

12 Charles Edmund Brock: pencil study for Mr Punch. Author's collection

15 © Vyara Boyadjieva www.vyaraboya.com @vyaraboya

16 Photo Bettina Strenske/imageBROKER/ Shutterstock

17 Cambridge School of Art archive

18 Ashmolean Museum, University of Oxford (WA1943.95). Photo Ashmolean Museum, University of Oxford/ Bridgeman Images

19 Ashmolean Museum, University of Oxford (WA1940.1.92). Photo Ashmolean Museum, University of Oxford/ Bridgeman Images

21 Museum of Modern Art, New York. Gift of Abby Aldrich Rockefeller (138.1940). Digital image, The Museum of Modern Art, New York/ Scala, Florence

23 © Michal Shalev

25–31 Courtesy Isabelle Arsenault

33 © The Ardizzone Trust. From *Jubilee: 1898-1948*, London, Camberwell School of Arts and Crafts, 1948

34 Heera Cha

35 Cambridge School of Art archive

36 al F Gregory Brown. London, Studio Publications, 1940

36 ar Artist unknown. Famous Art School Westport, Connecticut, 1964

37 al Artist unknown. Barcelona, Editorial Miguela A. Salvatella, undated

37 ar Artist unknown. Madrid, El Magisterial Español, 1935

39 a © The Ardizzone Trust, Private collection

39 b © The Ardizzone Trust. From *Brief to Council* by Henry Cecil. London: Michael Joseph, 1958

40 George Cruikshank, courtesy the Charles Dickens Museum, London

41 George Cruikshank. From *Oliver Twist* by Charles Dickens. London: Chapman & Hall, 1846

42 Courtesy the Lynton Lamb estate

43 © The Ardizzone Trust. Cairo, PR Publications ('for the Three Services in the Middle East'), 1942

44 © Martin Salisbury

47 © Estate of Feliks Topolski

48 © Martin Salisbury

49 © Estate of John Minton/Bridgeman Images

50–51 Cambridge School of Art archive

53 Cambridge School of Art archive. Photos by Martin Salisbury

55 Private collection, Vienna

56 Estate of Susan Einzig. Reproduction by kind permission of Hetty Einzig

59 © Pam Smy

60–61 © Seoungjun Baek

62–63 Cambridge School of Art archive

65 t Eric Hobbs, *Drawing for Advertising*. London: Studio Publications, 1956

66 © Martin Salisbury

67 © Anna Ring

68 t © Nastya Smirnova

68 b © Hye Young Kim

69 © Hanieh Ghashghaei

71–75 © Christopher Brown

77 From *Paul Hogarth's American Album: drawings, 1962–65* by Paul Hogarth. London: Lion and Unicorn Press, 1973. © Estate of Paul Hogarth

78 © Aude Van Ryn

79 © The Estate of Barbara Jones. From *Water-Colour Painting: A Practical Guide* by Barbara Jones. London: Adam and Charles Black, 1960

81 Gwen White. From *A Book of Pictorial Perspective* by Gwen White. London: John Murray, 1953

82–83 © Martin Salisbury

85 © Martin Salisbury

86–87 © Olga Shevchenko shevolya.com @shevolya_illustration

89 © Vyara Boyadjieva www.vyaraboya.com @vyaraboya

91 © Charlotte Bownass www.charlottebownass @charlottebownass

92 Sheila Robinson, by kind permission of Chloë Cheese and the Fry Art Gallery and Museum, Saffron Walden www.fryartgallery.org

93 © Jo Spooner www.jospoonerillustration.com @jojospooney

94–95 © Martin Salisbury

96, 97tl, 97 ar © Beatrice Alemagna

97 bl, 97 br © Angela Brooksbank

98–99 © Becky Brown www.becky-brown.com @beckybrownartandillustration

100 Cambridge School of Art archive

101 © Becky Brown

103 Courtesy of Bernie Fuchs Art, LLC and Courtesy of Taraba Illustration Art

104 © Becky Palmer www.beckypalmer.co.uk

107 © Kristin Roskifte www.kristinroskifte.no @kristin_roskifte

109 © The Ardizzone Trust. From *The Saturday Book*. London: Hutchinson, 1951

111–113 © Yann Kebbi

115 © Simon Bartram

117–120 © Bill Bragg @bill_bragg_illustration

121 From GHOSTLY TALES © 2017 Chronicle Books. Illustrated by Bill Bragg. Used with Permission from Chronicle Books, LLC. www.ChronicleBooks.com

123 © Nigel Robinson robinsonandwalsh@gmail.com

124–125 © Hayley Wells www.hayleywellsillustration.co.uk @hwillustrator

126 James Dawson. Author's collection

127 t © Gill Smith

127 b © Marina Ruiz Fernandez www.marinaruizillustration.com

129–131 © John Vernon Lord. Drawings from notebooks and diaries by John Vernon Lord (1976, 2002, 2004 and 2008). Published in *John's Journal Jottings*, Oxford: The Inky Parrot Press, 2009

133–135 © Sally Dunne

137–141 © Alexis Deacon. From *Soonchild* by Russell Hoban. London: Walker Books, 2012

142 Ronald Searle, Cambridge School of Art archive

145 © Jon McNaught. From *Dockwood* by Jon McNaught. London: Nobrow Ltd, 2012

147 Courtesy Emma Mason on behalf of the Robert Tavener estate

148–149 Trevor Willoughby, *Homes & Gardens*, Sept 1957

151–154 © David Humphries

157 Edward McKnight Kauffer © Simon Rendall

159–161 By kind permission of the Evelyn Dunbar estate

163–167 © Pablo Auladell www.pabloauladell.com @pabloauladell

169, 176–179 © Axel Scheffler

171–173 © Fifi Kuo

174–175 © Ellie Snowdon www.elliesnowdon.co.uk @snowdon_illo @esillustration

181 Arthur Rackham. From *Alice's Adventures in Wonderland*. London: William Heinemann, 1907
183–185 © Victoria Turnbull www.victurnbull.com @vic_turnbull
187–191 Sheila Robinson, by kind permission of Chloë Cheese and the Fry Art Gallery, www.fryartgallery.org
193 Winsor McCay. From *Little Nemo in Slumberland* (monthly strip), *New York Herald*, September 1907
195–197 © Isabel Greenberg. From *Glass Town*. London: Jonathan Cape, 2020 www.isabelgreenberg.co.uk @isabel_greenberg
199–201 © Jon McNaught. From *Kingdom*. London: Nobrow Ltd (2018)
203 Jules Chéret/Alamy Stock Photo
205 Photograph by Emma Brown Photography. Fabricators, *Riot of Colour* – Josh Mowll
206–207 ©Kerry Lemon www.kerrylemon.co.uk
209 Frank Newbould. From *Lesson Twenty-Three: Poster Drawing*, London: The British & Dominions School of Drawing, c. 1923
211 E H Shepard. Punch Cartoon Library/ TopFoto
213–215 © Paul Slater www.paulslater.me @paulslaterpics
217 © Laura Carlin

218-219 © 1946, 1986 All drawings reproduced with the kind permission of the Ronald Searle Cultural Trust and the Sayle Literary Agency
221–223 © David Hughes
225–227 Robert Weaver, sketchbook drawings
226 b From *Robert Weaver: A Pedestrian View: The Vogelman Diary* edited by Alexander Roob. Bönen, Germany: Kettler Verlag, February 28, 2013
229 © Estate of John Minton/Bridgeman Images
231 Printed by permission of the Norman Rockwell Family Agency. Copyright © 1951 the Norman Rockwell Family Entities
234 © The Ardizzone Trust. *Visiting Dieppe*, from *Signature: A Quadrimestrial of Typography and Graphic Arts*, No 13 (New Series), edited by Oliver Simon. London: Signature, 1951

ACKNOWLEDGMENTS

Thanks are due to the many, many people whose assistance and support has made this book possible, especially the students and immediate colleagues at Cambridge School of Art whose work has inspired and informed my own. At Thames & Hudson, I am especially grateful to editor Kate Edwards, designer Isabel Roldán, picture researcher Maria Ranauro and production controller Susanna Ingram. Further thanks go to my PhD students, Beatriz Lostalé Seijo and Flavia Zorilla Drago for their help with research. And finally, I am deeply indebted to all of the artists - students, graduates and professionals who have so generously allowed me to reproduce their work and who have taken time to share their thoughts and working practices.

INDEX

First published in the United Kingdom in 2022 by
Thames & Hudson Ltd, 181A High Holborn, London WC1V 7QX

First published in the United States of America in 2022 by
Thames & Hudson Inc., 500 Fifth Avenue, New York, New York 10110

British Library Cataloguing-in-Publication Data
A catalogue record for this book is available from the British Library

Library of Congress Control Number 2021943675

ISBN 978-0-500-02331-0

Printed and bound in China by C&C Offset Printing Co. Ltd

Be the first to know about our new releases,
exclusive content and author events by visiting
thamesandhudson.com
thamesandhudsonusa.com
thamesandhudson.com.au